THE
EVERYTHING®
EASY
VEGAN
COOKBOOK

Welcome to the Everything® Series!

These handy, accessible books give you all you need to tackle a difficult project, gain a new hobby, comprehend a fascinating topic, prepare for an exam, or even brush up on something you learned back in school but have since forgotten.

You can choose to read an Everything® book from cover to cover or just pick out the information you want from our four useful boxes: Questions, Facts, Alerts, and Essentials. We give you everything you need to know on the subject, but throw in a lot of fun stuff along the way too.

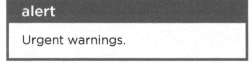

question

Answers to common questions.

fact

Important snippets of information.

alert

Urgent warnings.

essential

Quick handy tips.

We now have more than 600 Everything® books in print, spanning such wide-ranging categories as cooking, health, parenting, personal finance, wedding planning, word puzzles, and so much more. When you're done reading them all, you can finally say you know Everything®!

PUBLISHER Karen Cooper

MANAGING EDITOR Lisa Laing

COPY CHIEF Casey Ebert

PRODUCTION EDITOR Jo-Anne Duhamel

ACQUISITIONS EDITOR Lisa Laing

DEVELOPMENT EDITOR Lisa Laing

EVERYTHING® SERIES COVER DESIGNER Erin Alexander

THE
EVERYTHING®
EASY
VEGAN
COOKBOOK

**200 QUICK AND EASY RECIPES FOR
A HEALTHY, PLANT-BASED DIET**

ADAMS MEDIA

NEW YORK   LONDON   TORONTO   SYDNEY   NEW DELHI

Adams Media
An Imprint of Simon & Schuster, Inc.
100 Technology Center Drive
Stoughton, MA 02072

An Everything® Series Book.
Everything® and everything.com® are registered trademarks of Simon & Schuster, Inc.

First Adams Media trade paperback edition February 2021

ADAMS MEDIA and colophon are trademarks of Simon & Schuster.

For information about special discounts for bulk purchases, please contact Simon & Schuster Special Sales at 1-866-506-1949 or business@simonandschuster.com.

The Simon & Schuster Speakers Bureau can bring authors to your live event. For more information or to book an event contact the Simon & Schuster Speakers Bureau at 1-866-248-3049 or visit our website at www.simonspeakers.com.

Interior design by Colleen Cunningham
Interior photographs by James Stefiuk

Manufactured in the United States of America

2 2022

Library of Congress Cataloging-in-Publication Data has been applied for.

ISBN 978-1-5072-1563-0
ISBN 978-1-5072-1564-7 (ebook)

Contains material adapted from the following titles published by Adams Media, an Imprint of Simon & Schuster, Inc.: *The Everything® Vegan Cookbook* by Jolinda Hackett with Lorena Novak Bull, RD, copyright © 2010, ISBN 978-1-4405-0216-3; *The Everything® Vegan Meal Prep Cookbook* by Marly McMillen Beelman, copyright © 2019, ISBN 978-1-5072-1017-8; and *The Everything® Vegan Slow Cooker Cookbook* by Amy Snyder and Justin Snyder, copyright © 2012, ISBN 978-1-4405-4407-1.

Contents

7: RICE AND GRAINS   131

8: CLASSIC PASTAS   157

Introduction

People come to veganism for a variety of different reasons. Maybe you've been experimenting with vegetarianism or a plant-based diet to improve your health and want to take it a step further. Perhaps you're concerned about the toll meat production takes on the environment. Or you may want to avoid harming animals. Whatever your reason, you've come to the right place.

Whether you're a total newbie to the plant-based scene or someone who has been living the vegan lifestyle for years, *The Everything® Easy Vegan Cookbook* is here to guide you. The recipes in this book are designed to give you the opportunity to explore the many sides of vegan cooking. Start simply, with tofu breakfast scrambles or easy-to-assemble salads. Learn the basics of putting together a vegan soup, then experiment with a different combination of ingredients each time you make it. Try your hand at making nondairy milks, nut butters, or seitan from scratch. While the recipes are varied, they all have one thing in common—they're easy to make, and most of them are ready in 45 minutes or less.

A vegan diet has many health benefits. Eating vegan cuts out sources of LDL (or "bad") cholesterol and can lower your blood pressure, leading to better heart health. Veganism is also associated with a reduced risk of diabetes. Avoiding animal-based proteins can reduce the risk of some cancers as well. You may lose weight when you increase the number of whole foods you eat (like fruits, vegetables, whole grains, beans, and legumes) and reduce the amount of processed foods.

But don't worry—you won't feel deprived! Vegan cooking is all about showcasing and enhancing the wonderful variety of plant-based ingredients out there. Think sun-ripened tomatoes and juicy peaches, satisfying bean and grain bowls, and fresh, crunchy salads. And when you have a craving for a "cheesy" pasta bake or rich chocolate dessert, we've got you covered on that front too!

Read on to discover all you need to know about veganism and how to prepare hundreds of healthy, vibrant, and delicious dishes for any time of day. From Tofu Florentine (Chapter 3) to Sesame-Tahini Noodles (Chapter 8) to Maple Date Carrot Cake (Chapter 12), your new favorite recipes are waiting. Let's get started!

CHAPTER 1

The Vegan Revolution

If you're looking to eat healthier and feel better, veganism is the diet for you. It's true that there are restrictions with the vegan diet—but there are also a lot of benefits! Veganism is not just a diet, and not just the food on your plate. It's a method of preventive medicine, an active stance against environmental waste, and a boycott against animal cruelty. One small bite for you is one giant leap toward a healthier planet and a healthier body.

What Do Vegans Eat?

Eating a vegan diet essentially means that you don't consume products made from animals. Vegans don't eat meat, eggs, dairy, or other animal products, including honey. They also avoid animal by-products, such as gelatin.

> **fact**
>
> Gelatin is a protein derived from the skin, cartilage, and/or bones of animals. That means any product that uses gelatin, such as marshmallows, is not considered vegan. However, more and more companies are removing gelatin from their products, so check labels as you shop. There are also great plant-based alternatives to gelatin, such as agar-agar, which is derived from red algae.

That's a lot to take in. No ice cream? No scrambled eggs for breakfast? No sausage or pulled pork? No buttery biscuits with creamy gravy? This diet seems like a boring, restricted lifestyle. However, imagine this scenario: You sit down to a plate with a pulled "pork" barbecue sandwich and sides of French fries, coleslaw, and grilled corn on the cob. Afterward you enjoy a slice of chocolate layer cake with chocolate frosting and a scoop or two of ice cream. Does this sound like deprivation? No! And here's the kicker: It's all vegan.

Vegans eat mostly whole foods (fruits, vegetables, beans, nuts, grains) and dairy- and egg-free versions of traditional favorites (cheeseless pizza, bean burritos minus the cheese). Vegans enjoy hundreds of vegan substitute products, including nondairy cream cheese, "beef" jerky, and vegan white chocolate.

> **question**
>
> **Can I eat...?**
>
> Of course you *can*! Vegans *can* eat anything, but *choose* not to eat certain foods. When thinking about what to include and exclude in your diet, consider your reasons and values for choosing a vegan diet. Does eating a particular food align or conflict with these values? Whatever your diet may be, stick with your personal values and goals rather than dictionary definitions.

Vegan food has come a long way in recent years. While it was once a difficult undertaking to obtain vegan foods, they're now available in grocery stores and restaurants everywhere. Just about every comfort food has a vegan version. Each of the dozens of common substitutes, such as nondairy milk and vegan meats and cheeses, has its own texture and taste. The quality of vegan food products is much higher, too, which makes it tastier and easier than ever to go vegan!

Why Eat Vegan?

Ask a hundred vegans why they pass on animal foods and you may get a hundred different answers. Some do it for their health, for religious reasons, or to reduce animal suffering. Of course, being kind to our furry, feathery, and scaly friends is a big reason for eating vegan, but there are many other benefits, from helping the planet to preventing disease.

It's Good for the Environment

Every day you enjoy a vegan diet, you are saving over 1,000 gallons of water and over 30 square feet of forested land. Plants grow naturally with soil and sunshine, but animals require food—and a lot of it. The meat industry uses a lot more resources, like water, grains, and land, to produce less food when compared to the production of plant-based items like rice, beans, and vegetables. The waste emitted from meat production is also one of the largest contributors to global warming. In fact, the UN estimates that about 20 percent of all greenhouse gases comes from the food animal industry. By eliminating meat from your diet, you're reducing your carbon footprint and saving tons of environmental resources!

It Helps Animals

Billions of animals, including cows, pigs, and especially chickens, suffer because of the food industry each year. They don't spend their lives in idyllic pastures or in cute barns filled with bales of comfy hay. Instead, most animals raised to be consumed as food live out their lives in factory farms. On those factory farms, some animals are bred to grow so large that they cannot hold their own weight, and they may live out their days crammed into small, windowless spaces. There is little or no thought given to their well-being.

Many factory-farmed animals, including dairy cows and egg-laying chickens, live under these conditions. It's important to remember that animals that produce consumables often suffer just as much as animals that are directly consumed. Being vegan means that you avoid both of these types of products.

It's Good for Your Health

Recently, more people than ever are going vegan for their health, mind, and bodies, not just because of the cruelty to animals. Vegans, on average, weigh less than meat eaters, and they enjoy a reduced risk of heart disease and lower rates of diabetes. Additionally, vegans often report overall increased energy.

WEIGHT LOSS

The whole and plant-based foods provided in the vegan diet are a great start toward any weight loss goals! In fact, studies have shown that those who followed a vegan diet lost on average 5 pounds more than those who followed a standard omnivore diet. This is primarily because the vegan diet focuses on nutrient-dense ingredients such as greens, vegetables, beans, and nuts that promote weight loss.

Greens and vegetables are loaded with fiber, which improves your gut flora (microorganisms in the digestive tract that control metabolism) and helps you feel full longer. And many greens and vegetables are low in calories! Beans and nuts are also packed with healthy fiber, as well as protein that boosts metabolism and promotes muscle growth. In addition, nuts also contain healthy fats that can prevent belly fat.

> **essential**
>
> A vegan diet can be as healthy or as unhealthy as you make it. Focus on foods that feature filling, nutritious ingredients like beans, vegetables, fruits, and nuts that satisfy your daily nutritional needs. Make these part of your go-to favorite dishes, and then accessorize your meal plan with more indulgent vegan recipes like "pepperoni" or "sausage" pizza and carrot cake or chocolate chip cookies.

By skipping meat, dairy, and eggs when you eat, you are also skipping out on many unneeded calories in your diet. The average person needs roughly 2,000 calories per day, but most Americans are consuming far more than this. According to the Centers for Disease Control and Prevention, it is estimated that an alarming 36 percent of the population is now obese, and that number is only rising. Some people turn to diet pills or risky medical procedures for weight loss, but the solution can be much simpler—go vegan. While it is possible to be an obese vegan, because vegan foods are naturally lower in calories, it's not likely if you choose a healthy balanced diet.

HEART BENEFITS

The vegan diet is also good for your heart! Studies show that eating a vegan diet can lower your cholesterol and blood pressure levels, and balance your blood sugar levels.

Cholesterol is essential in building strong cells, promoting digestion, and enabling your body to produce vitamin D and certain hormones. Your body produces HDL ("good") cholesterol naturally, while LDL ("bad") cholesterol, which contributes to a number of health problems, is found in external sources such as meat, dairy, and processed foods. Vegans cut out those sources of bad cholesterol.

> **fact**
>
> Believe bad genes are out of your hands? The truth is that your genes are more closely tied to your diet than you may think! Dr. Dean Ornish, founder of Preventive Medicine Research Institute, discovered in his studies that being on a plant-based diet for just three months changed over 500 genes. Changes included turning on genes that prevent certain diseases and turning off genes that cause breast cancer and prostate cancer.

In addition, many studies have shown that consuming less meat helps maintain a healthy blood pressure, which is important in keeping arteries healthy and lessening the risk of stroke. Finally, a vegan diet helps balance your blood sugar, since the leading contributor to unbalanced blood sugar (refined sugar) is cut out or at least consumed in lower quantities.

Your cholesterol, blood pressure, and blood sugar levels are all important factors in heart health. An imbalance in any of these levels can cause serious issues such as diabetes or heart disease.

REDUCED RISK OF CANCER

Studies have also shown that those who eat a vegan diet also have a reduced risk of certain cancers (including breast, colon, and prostate cancer) compared to those who regularly eat meat. The main reason for this is that consumption of animal-based proteins such as beef and pork increases a cancer-promoting growth hormone called insulin-like growth factor 1 (IGF-1). IGF-1 is created naturally in the human body and is critical to development. However, when the body contains greater amounts, such as through eating meat, it can lead to the growth of cancerous cells.

In addition, the vegan diet focuses heavily on the consumption of vegetables, which contain a number of cancer-fighting substances such as carotenoids, beta-carotene, and flavones. These organic pigments are what give things like carrots their color. They also act as powerful antioxidants that combat the growth of cancerous cells while promoting the growth of healthy cells. Reducing or eliminating animal-based proteins from your diet, combined with an increased consumption of healthy vegetables and beans, is a prescription for a healthier life!

Vegan Nutrition

A vegan diet doesn't take more time and planning than a meat-filled diet, but a healthy, balanced diet does. If you don't put some thought into nutrition, then chances are you are not going to be eating a healthy, balanced diet, regardless of whether you are a vegan or a meat eater. Vegans are often questioned about nutrition, though, and are most often asked about where they get their protein. Most vegans easily meet their daily requirement of protein, but you should be aware of your mineral and vitamin (especially vitamin B_{12}) intake.

> **fact**
>
> Quinoa, soy, and hempseeds are vegan powerhouses when it comes to protein, as they contain the highest amount of all nine essential amino acids. Hempseeds are also high in omega-3 and omega-6 essential fatty acids.

Believe it or not, most Americans eat much more protein than recommended, and deficiency in vegans is rare. According to the Academy of Nutrition and Dietetics (formerly the American Dietetic Association), "Plant sources of protein alone can provide adequate amounts of the essential and nonessential amino acids, assuming that dietary protein sources from plants are reasonably varied." If, however, you tend to go weeks eating nothing but bananas and soda, you'll quickly find yourself deficient in more than just protein.

But eat a relatively healthy diet and you'll be just fine.

Though a vegan diet doesn't readily supply vitamin D, it's easily obtained from sunlight. Step outside for a few minutes a day and you're set for vitamin D. Make sure your vegan kids do the same. You could also rely on a daily supplement or fortified foods, such as fortified orange juice or soy milk.

Similarly, many soy foods are fortified with calcium, another important nutrient for dairy-free folks, and broccoli, tofu, tahini, almonds, and dark leafy greens provide a good natural source. But to build strong bones, you need exercise as well as calcium, so vegan or not, diet is only half the equation.

alert

Before you pour that glass of orange juice or soy milk, shake it up! The calcium in these drinks tends to settle to the bottom of the carton, so to get the best bone-boosting effect, shake before you drink.

When it comes to iron, most vegans and vegetarians actually get more than omnivores, but to be on the safe side, lentils, chickpeas, tahini, and once again, those dark leafy greens like spinach and kale are good vegan sources.

Noticing a pattern? Dark leafy green vegetables are one of the most nutrient-rich foods on the planet. Find ways to include kale, spinach, or other greens in your diet by snipping them into pasta sauces and casseroles, or include a few spinach leaves along with your other salad greens.

Fish oils and fish such as salmon are often touted as a source of healthy omega-3 fatty acids, but vegetarians and vegans can obtain these from flaxseeds and flax oil, as well as walnuts or hempseeds.

essential

Flaxseed oil is rich in omega-3s and has a sweet and nutty flavor. Never use flaxseed as a cooking oil, however—the heat destroys the healthy fats and creates unhealthy free radicals. Instead, add a teaspoonful of flaxseed oil to your favorite salad dressing, or drizzle over already cooked dishes for your daily omega-3s. Look for a brand that is cold-pressed, and store it in the refrigerator to keep it fresh.

Vitamin B_{12} can't be reliably obtained from vegan foods. Deficiencies of this important nutrient are very rare, and, if you're eating vegan meals only occasionally, you don't need to worry. Vegetarians will absorb B_{12} from food sources, but long-term vegans need a reliable source. Take a supplement and eat fortified foods, such as nutritional yeast.

Vegan Health Advantages

While B_{12} is a genuine concern, the health advantages of a plant-based diet are endless. The average vegan gets twice as much fiber as most omnivores. A vegan diet is naturally cholesterol-free and is almost guaranteed to lead to a decrease in your cholesterol levels in just two weeks. If lowering your cholesterol naturally is one of your goals, test your levels before and again a few weeks into a vegan diet, and gamble with your skeptical friends, just for fun.

Blood pressure, too, is shown to decrease drastically in a short period of time on a plant-based diet. High blood pressure is rarely a concern for vegans, and making the switch can decrease your blood pressure in less than two months. No need to give up salt as conventional wisdom dictates—just get rid of the meat and dairy!

You do need to eat a balanced diet in order to reap these benefits. After all, French fries and potato chips are animal-free, but that doesn't make them healthy. When it comes to vegan nutrition, variety is key. Make sure your protein sources are varied, rather than from just one food group. Eat a rainbow of fruits and veggies, and include green leafy vegetables as often as possible.

Going vegan won't make you look like your favorite Hollywood celebrity (who just might be vegan, too!) overnight, but with time you just might lose weight and improve your skin. Luckily, the advantages do not stop there, and there are many health benefits you'll experience by ditching meat, dairy, and eggs. Vegan diets are naturally:

- Low in calories
- Low in saturated fat
- Cholesterol-free
- High in vitamins and minerals

This means they are an excellent way to safeguard yourself against some unwanted diseases and weight gain.

How to Make the Switch

If you're not already a vegan, you may be wondering how to make the switch. Luckily, a plethora of resources (including this one!) are available to help you get started on your journey to a more compassionate lifestyle. You just need to decide which approach is best for you.

essential

There are two primary approaches to going vegan: cold turkey versus slowly easing in. Many people cannot eat another bite of nonvegan food once they learn about the conditions factory farm-raised animals endure, but for others, the transition is not so easy. For those people, it is recommended that they slowly phase out meats, then eggs, and then dairy, piece by piece, and replace them with vegan alternatives. If this method will help you stick with a vegan diet in the long run, then go for it and don't beat yourself up about not being able to jump right in.

Research

As a new vegan, one of the first things you will want to do is figure out what you can and cannot eat. It will usually be pretty obvious (no more hamburgers and pork hot dogs!), but at times, it isn't so clear-cut. PETA.org (www.peta.org) offers a list of ingredients that you may want to start looking out for when reading food labels. The names of these ingredients usually don't make it clear if a product is vegan or not. Don't obsess over getting this perfect, though, and know that if trace amounts of animal products slip into your diet, you are still doing more good than harm overall. Personal purity does not have to be your ultimate goal when switching to a vegan diet.

Experiment

Head out to your local grocery store, grab a cart, and start shopping, because experimenting with vegan food is the best part of becoming a vegan! Grocery store shelves are loaded with vegan cheeses, vegan mayonnaises, mock meats, and more. If you can't find the products you are looking for in the supermarket, head to the Internet. Some vegan food stores will deliver to your home!

Don't be afraid to try a recipe or ingredient you have not considered before. Many cookbooks and websites can help you plan your new vegan menu. If you aren't exactly an at-home chef, head out to your local restaurants to start experimenting with vegan cuisine. You'll find a diverse number of options depending on where you live, how much you want to spend, and what your tastes are.

Make Over Your Favorite Recipes

It's fairly easy to adapt traditional recipes to a vegan diet. With these recipes, most ingredients will stay the same. The protein and binding agents, such as eggs or cheese, will need to be replaced. Luckily, vegan substitutes for butter, cheese, milk, and a variety of meats are available in grocery stores nationwide, and you can substitute most without any special instructions. As you become more comfortable with a vegan diet, try reducing the amount of imitation products you use in favor of healthier whole foods such as tofu, tempeh, seitan, or beans. If you've never tried any of these ingredients, go ahead and add them to your favorite recipe to try out their interesting texture and get a vegan protein punch.

CHAPTER 2

Appetizers, Sauces, and Dips

Green and Black Olive Tapenade

MAKES 1 CUP

Per Serving (1 tablespoon):

Calories	34
Fat	3g
Sodium	180mg
Carbohydrates	1g
Fiber	1g
Sugar	0g
Protein	0g

Use tapenade as a topping for crostini or a dip with crackers and breadsticks. It also makes a lovely spread for a Mediterranean sandwich of grilled eggplant and zucchini.

½ cup pitted green olives
¾ cup pitted black olives
2 cloves garlic, peeled
1 tablespoon capers
2 tablespoons lemon juice
2 tablespoons olive oil
¼ teaspoon dried oregano
¼ teaspoon ground black pepper

1 Add all ingredients to a food processor. Process until almost smooth.
2 Transfer to a small bowl and serve immediately, or cover and refrigerate up to 1 week.

Roasted Red Pepper Hummus

As a dip or sandwich spread, hummus is always a favorite among vegans and nonvegans. Increase the garlic in this recipe if you're a garlic lover, or add crushed red pepper flakes for a zestier hummus.

1 (15-ounce) can chickpeas, drained and rinsed

⅓ cup tahini

⅔ cup chopped roasted red peppers

3 tablespoons lemon juice

2 tablespoons olive oil

2 cloves garlic, peeled

½ teaspoon ground cumin

¼ teaspoon salt

¼ teaspoon ground cayenne pepper

1 Add all ingredients to a blender or food processor. Process until smooth, scraping the sides down as needed.

2 Transfer to a small bowl and serve immediately, or cover and refrigerate up to 1 week.

MAKES 1½ CUPS

Per Serving (2 tablespoons):

Calories	91
Fat	6g
Sodium	163mg
Carbohydrates	8g
Fiber	2g
Sugar	2g
Protein	3g

DO-IT-YOURSELF ROASTED RED PEPPERS

Sure, you can buy them in a jar, but it's easy to roast your own. Here's how: Preheat your oven to 450°F (or use the broiler setting) and drizzle a few whole peppers with olive oil. Roast for 30 minutes or broil for 15 minutes, turning over once. Direct heat will also work, if you have a gas stove. Hold the peppers with tongs over the flame until lightly charred. Let the peppers cool, then remove the skin.

Baba Ghanoush

MAKES 1½ CUPS

Per Serving (¼ cup):

Calories	159
Fat	11g
Sodium	114mg
Carbohydrates	13g
Fiber	6g
Sugar	6g
Protein	3g

Whip up a batch of Baba Ghanoush along with Roasted Red Pepper Hummus and Vegan Tzatziki (see recipes in this chapter) for a Mediterranean appetizer spread. Don't forget to add some vegan pita bread for dipping.

2 medium eggplants, trimmed and sliced in half lengthwise

3 tablespoons olive oil, divided

2 tablespoons lemon juice

¼ cup tahini

3 cloves garlic, peeled and minced

½ teaspoon ground cumin

½ teaspoon chili powder

¼ teaspoon salt

1 tablespoon chopped fresh parsley

1 Preheat oven to 400°F. Prick eggplants several times with a fork.

2 Place cut-side up on a large baking sheet and drizzle with 1 tablespoon olive oil. Bake 30 minutes or until soft. Set aside 10 minutes to cool slightly. Scoop out the inner flesh of the eggplants and place in a large bowl.

3 Using a large fork or potato masher, mash eggplant together with remaining ingredients until almost smooth. Transfer to a small bowl and serve immediately.

Homemade Tahini

If you're serving this as a dip or spread, use the paprika for extra flavor and color, but leave it out if your tahini will be the basis for a salad dressing or a noodle dish.

2 cups sesame seeds
½ cup olive oil
½ teaspoon paprika

1 Preheat oven to 350°F.
2 Spread sesame seeds in a thin layer on a baking sheet and toast 5 minutes in the oven, shaking the sheet once to mix. Set aside to cool 5 minutes.
3 Place sesame seeds and oil in a food processor or blender and process until thick and creamy. You may need a little more or less than ½ cup oil.
4 Garnish with paprika before serving. Tahini will keep up to 1 month in the refrigerator in a tightly sealed container, or frozen up to 3 months.

MAKES 1 CUP

Per Serving (1 tablespoon):

Calories	162
Fat	15g
Sodium	2mg
Carbohydrates	4g
Fiber	2g
Sugar	0g
Protein	3g

Fresh Mint Spring Rolls

DIP OPTIONS

Store-bought sweet chili sauce, sriracha sauce, or a sesame-ginger salad dressing or marinade will work as a dip for spring rolls, but you can make your own. Try the Thai Orange-Peanut Dressing (see recipe in Chapter 4) or Easy Asian Dipping Sauce (see recipe in this chapter).

Wrapping spring rolls is a balance between getting them tight enough to hold together, but not so tight the thin wrappers break! It's like riding a bike: Once you've got it, you've got it, and then spring rolls are quick and fun to make.

1 (3-ounce) package clear bean thread noodles

1 cup hot water

1 tablespoon soy sauce

½ teaspoon ground ginger

1 teaspoon sesame oil

¼ cup diced shiitake mushrooms

1 medium carrot, peeled and grated

12 spring roll wrappers

½ medium head green leaf lettuce, cored and chopped

1 small cucumber, thinly sliced

1 bunch fresh mint

1 Break noodles in half and place in a medium bowl. Cover with 1 cup hot water and set aside until soft, 6–7 minutes. Drain and transfer to a large bowl.

2 Add soy sauce, ginger, sesame oil, mushrooms, and carrot and toss to combine.

3 In a large shallow pan, carefully submerge one spring roll wrapper in warm water until just barely soft. Remove from water and place on a flat surface.

4 Place a bit of lettuce in the center of the wrapper. Add about 2 tablespoons noodle mixture, a few slices of cucumber, and 2–3 mint leaves. Fold the bottom of the wrapper over the filling, fold in each side, then roll. Repeat with remaining ingredients.

5 Serve immediately.

Easy Asian Dipping Sauce

MAKES ⅓ CUP

Per Serving (1 tablespoon):

Calories	27
Fat	2g
Sodium	657mg
Carbohydrates	2g
Fiber	0g
Sugar	1g
Protein	1g

Tangy, salty, spicy, and a bit sour—this easy dipping sauce has it all! Use it for dipping vegan sushi or Fresh Mint Spring Rolls (see recipe in this chapter). It would also make an excellent marinade for baked tofu.

¼ **cup soy sauce**

2 **tablespoons rice vinegar**

2 **teaspoons sesame oil**

1 **teaspoon sugar**

1 **teaspoon minced fresh ginger**

2 **cloves garlic, peeled and minced**

¼ **teaspoon crushed red pepper flakes**

In a small bowl, add all ingredients and whisk together until combined.

Vegan Mayonnaise

The secret to getting a really creamy homemade Vegan Mayonnaise is to add the oil very, very slowly—literally just a few drops at a time—and use the highest speed on your food processor.

1 (12-ounce) package silken tofu, drained

1½ tablespoons lemon juice

1 teaspoon prepared mustard

1½ teaspoons apple cider vinegar or distilled white vinegar

1 teaspoon sugar

¾ teaspoon onion powder

½ teaspoon salt

⅓ cup canola oil or safflower oil

1 Add tofu, lemon juice, mustard, vinegar, sugar, onion powder, and salt to a food processor. Process until smooth.

2 On high speed, continue to process as you slowly incorporate the oil a few drops at a time until smooth and creamy.

3 Refrigerate at least 1 hour before using to allow flavors to blend. Mayonnaise will also thicken as it sits.

MAKES 1 CUP

Per Serving (1 tablespoon):

Calories	57
Fat	5g
Sodium	121mg
Carbohydrates	1g
Fiber	0g
Sugar	1g
Protein	2g

FROM THOUSAND ISLAND TO AIOLI

Mayonnaise is used in so many comfort foods that you'll really want to have a good one on hand most of the time. Making your own is easy, but many options are available in your grocery store. Try out a few and find your favorite.

Vegan "Pigs" in a Blanket

SERVES 16

Per Serving:

Calories	101
Fat	2g
Sodium	409mg
Carbohydrates	15g
Fiber	1g
Sugar	1g
Protein	5g

PARTY PIGS

If you go to enough parties, you'll inevitably run into a variation of this recipe sooner or later—it's an old vegan favorite. Add some extra flavor to the "pigs" before rolling them up—try a bit of vegan cheese, a squirt of mustard, or a generous sprinkle of crushed red pepper flakes.

This is a great little appetizer that both kids and adults love. Serve them with ketchup or hot mustard. If you're short on time, use store-bought vegan crescent roll dough.

1 batch Quick and Easy Vegan Biscuits dough (see recipe in Chapter 3)

8 vegan hot dogs, sliced in half

1 Preheat oven to 400°F. Lightly grease a large baking sheet.
2 Divide dough into sixteen pieces and roll into ovals.
3 Place a hot dog half on the edge of a dough oval and roll, leaving the ends open. Place on prepared baking sheet. Repeat with remaining dough and hot dogs.
4 Bake 10–12 minutes or until lightly golden brown. Serve hot.

Nacho "Cheese" Dip

Peanut butter in "cheese" sauce? No, that's not a typo! A little peanut butter adds a creamy and nutty layer of flavor to this sauce and helps it to thicken nicely. Use the sauce to dress plain steamed vegetables or make homemade nachos.

3 tablespoons vegan margarine

1 cup unsweetened soy milk

¾ teaspoon garlic powder

½ teaspoon salt

½ teaspoon onion powder

1 tablespoon smooth peanut butter

¼ cup all-purpose flour

¼ cup nutritional yeast

¾ cup bottled salsa

2 tablespoons chopped canned jalapeño peppers

1 In a small saucepan over low heat, heat margarine and soy milk together until margarine melts, about 3 minutes. Add garlic powder, salt, and onion powder and stir to combine. Add peanut butter and stir 2 minutes until melted.

2 Whisk in flour, 1 tablespoon at a time, until smooth. Heat 5–6 minutes until thickened.

3 Stir in yeast, salsa, and jalapeño peppers.

4 Transfer to a small bowl and let cool slightly before serving. The dip will thicken as it cools.

MAKES 1 CUP

Per Serving (¼ cup):

Calories	135
Fat	7g
Sodium	731mg
Carbohydrates	13g
Fiber	3g
Sugar	3g
Protein	6g

CHILI CHEESE

Add a can of store-bought vegan chili to make a chili-cheese dip to serve with hearty corn chips. Or pour it over a pile of French fries for the ultimate comfort food.

Mango-Citrus Salsa

Salsa has a variety of uses, and this recipe adds color and variety to your usual chips and dip or Mexican dishes.

1 medium mango, peeled, pitted, and chopped

2 small tangerines, peeled and chopped

½ medium red bell pepper, seeded and chopped

½ small red onion, peeled and minced

3 cloves garlic, peeled and minced

½ small jalapeño pepper, seeded and minced

2 tablespoons lime juice

½ teaspoon salt

¼ teaspoon ground black pepper

3 tablespoons chopped fresh cilantro

1 In a medium bowl, add all ingredients. Gently toss together to combine.

2 Set aside at least 15 minutes before serving to allow flavors to mingle.

MAKES 2 CUPS

Per Serving (¼ cup):

Calories	42
Fat	0g
Sodium	146mg
Carbohydrates	10g
Fiber	1g
Sugar	8g
Protein	1g

Mushroom Gravy

MAKES 1½ CUPS

Per Serving (¼ cup):

Calories	60
Fat	3g
Sodium	583mg
Carbohydrates	6g
Fiber	1g
Sugar	1g
Protein	1g

The secret to perfect vegan gravy, like regular gravy, is in the stirring, to prevent lumps. Mushrooms and herbs add hefty flavors to this savory gravy.

¼ cup vegan margarine
¾ cup sliced mushrooms
2½ cups vegetable broth
1 teaspoon garlic powder
1 teaspoon onion powder
½ teaspoon ground sage
½ teaspoon dried thyme
¼ teaspoon ground marjoram
3 tablespoons all-purpose flour
2 tablespoons nutritional yeast
½ teaspoon salt
½ teaspoon ground black pepper

1 In a large skillet over medium heat, heat margarine. Add mushrooms and sauté 2–3 minutes until soft.
2 Reduce heat to medium-low and add broth, garlic powder, onion powder, sage, thyme, and marjoram, stirring to combine.
3 Add flour, 1 tablespoon at a time, whisking constantly to combine and prevent lumps from forming. Cook 2–3 minutes until flour is fully incorporated. Continue simmering over low heat about 3 minutes until thickened.
4 Remove from heat and stir in yeast, salt, and pepper. Cool slightly before serving; gravy will thicken as it cools.

Tropical Cashew Nut Butter

You can make a homemade cashew nut butter with any kind of oil, so feel free to substitute whatever you have on hand. But you're in for a real treat when you use coconut oil in this recipe!

2 cups roasted cashews
½ teaspoon sugar
¼ teaspoon salt
3 tablespoons coconut oil or other vegetable oil

1 Add cashews, sugar, and salt to a food processor. Process on high speed until finely ground. Continue processing until the mixture forms a thick paste.

2 Slowly add coconut oil until smooth and creamy, scraping down sides and adding a little more oil if needed.

3 Serve immediately or transfer to a covered container. Cashew butter will keep at room temperature for up to 2 months or in the refrigerator for up to 6 months.

MAKES ¾ CUP

Per Serving (2 tablespoons):

Calories	241
Fat	20g
Sodium	78mg
Carbohydrates	11g
Fiber	1g
Sugar	2g
Protein	5g

MAKING NUT BUTTERS

Nut butters can be expensive to buy at the store, but they're so easy to make at home! Try making almond, walnut, or macadamia nut butter for a delicious alternative to plain old peanut butter. Roasted nuts work best, so heat them in the oven at 400°F 6–8 minutes or toast them on the stovetop in a dry skillet over medium heat for a few minutes.

Sun-Dried Tomato Pesto

MAKES 1 CUP

Per Serving (2 tablespoons):

Calories	132
Fat	12g
Sodium	154mg
Carbohydrates	4g
Fiber	1g
Sugar	1g
Protein	3g

BEYOND PESTO PASTA

Pesto is a simple sauce, but it can be used in a variety of different ways. It's not just for tossing with pasta—serve it with whole-grain crackers as an appetizer, use it as a sandwich spread, or spread it on vegan focaccia for the base of a delicious vegan pizza. You can even turn it into a creamy dip by mixing it with a container of nondairy sour cream.

Nutritional yeast lends a strong cheesy flavor to this vegan pesto, and the sun-dried tomatoes add another layer of flavor to the traditional basil. Don't tell anyone it's vegan, and they might never know!

⅓ cup sun-dried tomatoes (not packed in oil)

2 cups fresh basil leaves

½ cup pine nuts or walnuts

3 cloves garlic, peeled

¼ cup nutritional yeast

½ teaspoon salt

¼ teaspoon ground black pepper

¼ cup olive oil

1 In a small bowl, place sun-dried tomatoes and cover with water. Let stand about 15 minutes until soft and pliable. Drain, then transfer to a food processor or blender.

2 Add basil, nuts, garlic, yeast, salt, and pepper. Process until the mixture is puréed. With the motor running, slowly add oil to achieve desired consistency.

3 Serve immediately or transfer to a covered container and refrigerate up to 1 week.

Vegan Tzatziki

Use a vegan soy yogurt to make this classic Greek dip, which is best served very cold. A nondairy sour cream may be used instead of the soy yogurt, if you prefer.

1½ cups plain vegan soy yogurt

1 tablespoon olive oil

1 tablespoon lemon juice

4 cloves garlic, peeled and minced

2 small cucumbers, peeled and grated

1 tablespoon chopped fresh mint or dill

1 In a small bowl, add yogurt, olive oil, and lemon juice. Whisk until combined.

2 Stir in remaining ingredients.

3 Refrigerate at least 1 hour before serving to allow flavors to mingle. Serve cold.

MAKES 1½ CUPS

Per Serving (2 tablespoons):

Calories	45
Fat	1g
Sodium	5mg
Carbohydrates	7g
Fiber	1g
Sugar	3g
Protein	1g

Scallion Pancakes

SERVES 6

Per Serving:

Calories	232
Fat	9g
Sodium	196mg
Carbohydrates	33g
Fiber	2g
Sugar	0g
Protein	5g

These salty fried pancakes are a popular street food snack in East Asia. Plain soy sauce is the perfect dip.

2 cups all-purpose flour

½ teaspoon salt

¾ cup hot water

4 teaspoons sesame oil, divided

6 scallions, trimmed and chopped (green parts only)

¼ cup vegetable oil

1 In a large bowl, combine flour and salt. Slowly add water and 2 teaspoons sesame oil, mixing just until a dough forms. You may need a little bit less than ¾ cup water.

2 Knead dough for 3 minutes, then set aside for 30 minutes.

3 Divide dough into six (2") balls. On a lightly floured surface, roll out each ball to a disk ½" thick. Brush a disk with 1 teaspoon sesame oil and cover with half of the scallions. Roll up dough and twist to form a ball. Roll out again into a disk ¼" thick. Repeat with remaining dough, oil, and scallions.

4 Line a large plate with paper towels.

5 In a large skillet, heat vegetable oil over medium-high heat. Fry each pancake 1–2 minutes on each side. Transfer to lined plate to drain.

6 Slice pancakes into squares or wedges and serve warm or at room temperature.

Vegan Chocolate-Hazelnut Spread

Per Serving (1 tablespoon):

Calories	145
Fat	12g
Sodium	0mg
Carbohydrates	9g
Fiber	2g
Sugar	5g
Protein	3g

BESIDES JUST LICKING THE SPOON...

Europeans spread it on toast, Asian teenagers spread it on pancakes and stuff it inside waffles, but you can use it however you want—use it to top Vegan Crepes (see recipe in Chapter 3) for dessert, spread it over apple slices for the kids, or, go ahead, just eat it plain! If you can't find hazelnuts, cashews will work well to make a creamy spread.

Treat yourself or your family with this rich, sticky chocolate spread. Be warned—everyone will want to lick the spoon!

2 cups chopped hazelnuts
½ cup unsweetened cocoa powder
¾ cup confectioners' sugar
½ teaspoon vanilla extract
4 tablespoons vegetable oil

1 Process hazelnuts in a food processor 3–4 minutes until very finely ground. Add cocoa powder, confectioners' sugar, and vanilla and pulse to combine.

2 Add oil, a little bit at a time, until mixture is soft and creamy and desired consistency is reached. You may need to add a bit more or less than 4 tablespoons.

Spicy Basil and Roasted Cashew Pesto

The combination of spicy holy basil (in place of the traditional Italian sweet basil) and the bite of the garlic creates an electrifying vegan pesto.

4 cloves garlic, peeled

1 cup Thai basil or holy basil leaves, packed

⅔ cup roasted cashews

½ cup nutritional yeast

¾ teaspoon salt

½ teaspoon ground black pepper

⅓ cup olive oil

1 Add garlic, basil, cashews, yeast, salt, and pepper to a blender or food processor. Pulse just until coarse and combined.

2 With the motor running, slowly add oil until desired consistency is reached. You may need slightly more or less oil than ⅓ cup.

3 Serve immediately or transfer to a covered container and refrigerate up to 1 week.

SERVES 3

Per Serving:

Calories	434
Fat	37g
Sodium	603mg
Carbohydrates	15g
Fiber	3g
Sugar	2g
Protein	11g

TRADITIONAL PESTO

For a more traditional Italian pesto, you can, of course, use sweet Italian basil. If you do, cut back on the garlic a bit and use pine nuts or walnuts instead of cashews.

Quick Hollandaise Sauce

MAKES ½ CUP

Per Serving (2 tablespoons):

Calories	143
Fat	13g
Sodium	560mg
Carbohydrates	2g
Fiber	0g
Sugar	1g
Protein	1g

NONDAIRY MILKS

Soy and almond milk are no longer the only options for dairy-free milks. In most grocery stores, you'll find oat milk, rice milk, hemp milk, cashew milk, and macadamia milk. For baking, soy or almond milk is best. Mild oat milk is good in cereal and smoothies. Rice and hemp milks are thinner than the richer cashew and macadamia nut milks. Read the labels; there is a lot of variation in calorie count and fat, protein, and carbohydrate content. Some varieties are also fortified with nutrients found in cow's milk, like vitamin D, B_{12}, and calcium.

A classic hollandaise sauce is made from raw eggs, but this vegan version uses prepared vegan mayonnaise with a bit of turmeric for a yellow hue. Pour it over steamed asparagus, artichokes, or cauliflower for an easy side dish, or make a Tofu Florentine (see recipe in Chapter 3) or "eggs" Benedict.

⅓ cup vegan mayonnaise

¼ cup lemon juice

3 tablespoons unsweetened soy milk

1½ tablespoons Dijon mustard

¼ teaspoon ground turmeric

1 tablespoon nutritional yeast

½ teaspoon salt

¼ teaspoon ground black pepper

¼ teaspoon hot sauce

1 In a small saucepan over medium heat, combine all ingredients. Whisk constantly until mixture thickens, about 5 minutes.

2 Serve immediately.

CHAPTER 3

Breakfast

Chili Masala Tofu Scramble

SERVES 2

Per Serving:

Calories	314
Fat	21g
Sodium	471mg
Carbohydrates	15g
Fiber	5g
Sugar	6g
Protein	20g

THE NEXT DAY

Leftover tofu scramble makes an excellent lunch, or you can wrap leftovers in warmed flour tortillas to make breakfast-style burritos—just add salsa or beans.

Tofu scramble is an easy and versatile vegan breakfast. This version adds chili and curry for an Indian flavor. Toss in whatever vegetables you have on hand—chopped tomatoes, spinach, or broccoli would work well.

2 tablespoons olive oil

1 small onion, peeled and diced

2 cloves garlic, peeled and minced

1 (14-ounce) package firm or extra-firm tofu, drained, pressed, and chopped into 1" pieces

1 small red chili pepper, seeded and minced

1 medium green bell pepper, seeded and chopped

¾ cup sliced mushrooms

1 tablespoon soy sauce

1 teaspoon curry powder

½ teaspoon ground cumin

¼ teaspoon ground turmeric

1 teaspoon nutritional yeast

1 In a large skillet, heat oil over medium-high heat. Add onion and garlic and sauté 4–5 minutes until soft.

2 Stir in tofu, chili pepper, bell pepper, mushrooms, soy sauce, curry powder, cumin, and turmeric. Sauté 6–8 minutes until tofu is lightly browned.

3 Remove from heat and stir in nutritional yeast. Serve immediately.

Vegan Pancakes

Just half a banana and a tablespoon of sugar add body to the batter for perfectly fluffy pancakes. Serve them with fresh fruit and a sprinkle of confectioners' sugar or drizzle them with pure maple syrup.

1 cup all-purpose flour

1 tablespoon sugar

1¾ teaspoons baking powder

¼ teaspoon salt

½ medium banana, peeled

1 teaspoon vanilla extract

1 cup unsweetened soy milk

1 In a large bowl, mix together flour, sugar, baking powder, and salt.

2 In a separate small bowl, mash banana with a fork. Add vanilla and whisk until smooth and fluffy. Add soy milk and stir to combine well.

3 Add soy milk mixture to flour mixture, stirring just until combined.

4 Heat a lightly greased griddle or large skillet over medium heat. Drop batter about 3 tablespoons at a time and cook 2–3 minutes until bubbles appear on surface. Flip and cook other side another 1–2 minutes until lightly golden brown. Repeat with remaining batter.

5 Serve immediately.

SERVES 4

Per Serving:

Calories	167
Fat	0g
Sodium	388mg
Carbohydrates	33g
Fiber	1g
Sugar	7g
Protein	5g

DON'T OVERMIX!

When it comes to mixing pancake batter, less is more! Pancakes should be light and fluffy, but overmixing the batter will make them tough and rubbery. Gently combine the wet ingredients with the dry ones and don't be afraid of a few lumps; they'll sort themselves out when heated.

Carob, Peanut Butter, and Banana Smoothie

Good enough for a dessert, but healthy enough for breakfast, this smoothie is also a satisfying protein boost after a sweaty workout at the gym. Use unsweetened cocoa powder if you don't have carob.

8 ice cubes
2 medium bananas, peeled
2 tablespoons peanut butter
2 tablespoons carob powder
1 cup unsweetened soy milk

Place all ingredients in a blender and process until smooth. Divide between two glasses and serve immediately.

SERVES 2

Per Serving:

Calories	290
Fat	8g
Sodium	66mg
Carbohydrates	43g
Fiber	5g
Sugar	24g
Protein	9g

Avocado Toast

SERVES 4

Per Serving:

Calories	199
Fat	10g
Sodium	442mg
Carbohydrates	20g
Fiber	7g
Sugar	2g
Protein	6g

Healthy recipes don't get much easier than this. Start with the basic recipe, then experiment with additional toppings, like diced tomatoes, chopped walnuts, or sliced mushrooms.

2 medium avocados, peeled, halved, and pitted

1 tablespoon nutritional yeast

½ teaspoon salt

¼ teaspoon ground black pepper

1 teaspoon lemon juice

½ teaspoon dried chives

4 slices whole-wheat bread

1 clove garlic, peeled and halved

1 Spoon avocado flesh into a medium bowl. Add yeast, salt, pepper, lemon juice, and chives and mash together, using a fork to create a slightly chunky mixture.
2 Toast bread 4 minutes or until lightly browned.
3 While toast is still warm, rub cut side of halved garlic clove across one side of each toast slice.
4 Spread avocado mixture over toast and serve.

Vanilla-Date Breakfast Smoothie

Adding dates to a basic soy milk and fruit smoothie adds a blast of unexpected sweetness. It makes a healthy breakfast treat or a cooling summer snack.

4 large dates, pitted

¾ cup unsweetened soy milk

2 medium bananas, peeled

6 ice cubes

¼ teaspoon vanilla extract

1 Place dates in a small bowl and cover with water. Set aside to soak at least 10 minutes. Drain and transfer dates to a blender.

2 Add remaining ingredients to blender and process on medium speed about 1 minute until smooth. Serve immediately.

SERVES 2

Per Serving:

Calories	276
Fat	1g
Sodium	46mg
Carbohydrates	66g
Fiber	7g
Sugar	49g
Protein	5g

A SMOOTHER SMOOTHIE

Soaking the dates first will help them process a little quicker and results in a smoother consistency. Of course, you can make the smoothie without soaking the dates. The texture will just be a little grainier.

Blueberry Overnight Oats

SERVES 2

Per Serving:

Calories	259
Fat	9g
Sodium	1mg
Carbohydrates	38g
Fiber	8g
Sugar	6g
Protein	8g

Combine the ingredients for overnight oats on a Sunday night and enjoy a tasty, healthy, and easy breakfast later in the week.

1 cup rolled oats, divided

1 tablespoon chia seeds

2 tablespoons sliced almonds

1½ cups water

2 teaspoons stevia

1 teaspoon vanilla extract

½ cup fresh blueberries, divided

1 tablespoon granola

1 Place 1 tablespoon oats, chia seeds, almonds, water, stevia, and vanilla in a blender. Blend until smooth. Add ¼ cup blueberries and pulse until smooth.

2 Place remaining oats in a medium bowl. Pour blueberry mixture over oats. Stir to combine. Divide mixture between two small sealed containers. Refrigerate at least 2 hours or up to 5 days.

3 Remove from refrigerator and top with granola and remaining ¼ cup blueberries before serving.

Strawberry Protein Smoothie

Silken tofu added to a simple fruit smoothie makes a creamy, satisfying drink with a healthy protein boost.

½ cup frozen unsweetened strawberries

½ (14-ounce) package silken tofu, drained

1 medium banana, peeled

¾ cup orange juice

3–4 ice cubes

1 tablespoon agave nectar

1 Place all ingredients in a blender and blend until smooth and creamy.

2 Divide between two glasses and serve immediately.

SERVES 2

Per Serving:

Calories	193
Fat	3g
Sodium	38mg
Carbohydrates	35g
Fiber	3g
Sugar	23g
Protein	8g

PROTEIN SHAKES

While many protein powders contain dairy or egg-based ingredients, many are naturally vegan. Look for powders made with pea protein, hemp protein powder, or flax meal. A scoop of one of these powders in a smoothie will give you an extra protein punch.

Vegan Crepes

IT'S ALL IN THE WRIST

Don't worry if the first one or two crepes turn out less than perfect; it always seems to happen. As you master the swirl technique, you'll soon be churning out perfect crepes every time. If you've never tried, you may want to make a double batch so you can practice. Be sure to use a nonstick pan!

Crepes make a lovely brunch or even dessert, depending on what you fill them with. Try fresh berries, sliced peaches, or a crunchy nut butter.

1 cup all-purpose flour

¾ cup unsweetened soy milk

¼ cup water

2 teaspoons sugar

1 teaspoon vanilla extract

¼ cup melted vegan margarine

¼ teaspoon salt

1 In a medium bowl, whisk together all ingredients. Cover bowl and refrigerate at least 1 hour. Remove from refrigerator and stir.

2 Lightly grease a large nonstick skillet and heat over medium-high heat.

3 Place about ¼ cup batter in skillet and swirl to coat the bottom of the skillet. Cook 1 minute until set, then carefully flip, using a spatula or even your hands. Heat 1 more minute, then transfer to a plate.

4 Repeat with remaining batter. Serve immediately.

Vanilla Flax Granola

MAKES 2½ CUPS

Per Serving (½ cup):

Calories	413
Fat	11g
Sodium	94mg
Carbohydrates	73g
Fiber	7g
Sugar	41g
Protein	7g

Making your own granola lets you add whatever flavors you like. Try crystallized ginger, chopped dates, a sprinkle of cinnamon, coconut flakes, dried papaya—the possibilities are endless!

⅔ cup maple syrup

⅓ cup vegan margarine

1½ teaspoons vanilla extract

2 cups rolled oats

½ cup flax meal or wheat germ

¾ cup raisins or dried cranberries

1 Preheat oven to 325°F.

2 In a small saucepan over low heat, whisk together syrup, margarine, and vanilla until margarine is melted.

3 On a large baking sheet, toss together oats, flax meal, and raisins in a single layer.

4 Drizzle maple syrup mixture over oat mixture, gently tossing to combine.

5 Bake 25–30 minutes, carefully stirring once during cooking. Let cool on baking sheet at least 30 minutes before serving.

6 Granola can be stored in an airtight container in a cool, dry place up to 1 month.

Apple-Cinnamon Waffles

For perfect vegan waffles, make sure your waffle iron is hot and very well greased, because vegan waffles tend to be stickier than regular waffles.

1¼ cups all-purpose flour

2 teaspoons baking powder

½ teaspoon ground cinnamon

2 teaspoons sugar

1 cup unsweetened soy milk

½ cup applesauce

1 teaspoon vanilla extract

1 tablespoon vegetable oil

1 Thoroughly grease a waffle iron and preheat.
2 In a large bowl, combine flour, baking powder, cinnamon, and sugar. Set aside.
3 In a separate small bowl, combine soy milk, applesauce, vanilla, and oil.
4 Add soy milk mixture to flour mixture, stirring just until combined; do not overmix.
5 Carefully drop about ¼ cup batter onto hot waffle iron. Close and cook according to manufacturer's directions. Repeat with remaining batter.
6 Serve immediately.

SERVES 4

Per Serving:

Calories	231
Fat	4g
Sodium	274mg
Carbohydrates	40g
Fiber	2g
Sugar	8g
Protein	6g

Whole-Wheat Blueberry Muffins

MAKES 18 MUFFINS

Per Serving (1 muffin):

Calories	147
Fat	0g
Sodium	220mg
Carbohydrates	33g
Fiber	2g
Sugar	17g
Protein	3g

VEGAN MUFFINS

You can probably turn any family-favorite muffin recipe into a vegan version. Use a commercial egg replacer in place of the eggs, and substitute vegan margarine and nondairy milk for the butter and milk.

Because these muffins have very little fat, they'll want to stick to the papers or the muffin tin. Letting them cool before removing them will help prevent this.

2 cups whole-wheat flour

1 cup all-purpose flour

1¼ cups sugar

1 tablespoon baking powder

1 teaspoon salt

1½ cups unsweetened soy milk

½ cup applesauce

½ teaspoon vanilla extract

2 cups blueberries, divided

1 Preheat oven to 400°F. Grease eighteen muffin tin cups or line them with paper liners.

2 In a large bowl, combine whole-wheat flour, all-purpose flour, sugar, baking powder, and salt. Set aside.

3 In a separate small bowl, whisk together soy milk, applesauce, and vanilla. Add to flour mixture and stir just until combined; do not overmix.

4 Gently fold in 1 cup blueberries.

5 Spoon batter into prepared muffin tins, filling each cup about two-thirds full. Sprinkle remaining blueberries on top of muffins.

6 Bake 20–25 minutes until lightly golden brown on top. Allow to cool in muffin cups 5 minutes before serving.

Quick and Easy Vegan Biscuits

Use these vegan biscuits to soak up Mushroom Gravy (see recipe in Chapter 2) or make Vegan "Pigs" in a Blanket (see recipe in Chapter 2). Top them with vegan margarine for breakfast.

2 cups all-purpose flour

1 tablespoon baking powder

½ teaspoon onion powder

½ teaspoon garlic powder

½ teaspoon salt

5 tablespoons cold vegan margarine

⅔ cup unsweetened soy milk

1 Preheat oven to 425°F.
2 In a large bowl, stir together flour, baking powder, onion powder, garlic powder, and salt until combined. Add margarine.
3 Using a fork or pastry blender, mash margarine into the flour mixture until mixture is crumbly. Add soy milk a few tablespoons at a time and combine just until dough forms. You may need to add a little more or less than ⅔ cup.
4 Knead a few times on a floured surface, then roll out to ¾" thick. Cut into 3" rounds. Reroll scraps and cut more biscuits until dough is used up.
5 Place rounds on a large ungreased baking sheet about 1" apart. Bake 12–14 minutes until lightly browned.
6 Serve immediately or store covered up to 1 week in the refrigerator.

SERVES 12

Per Serving:

Calories	102
Fat	2g
Sodium	259mg
Carbohydrates	17g
Fiber	1g
Sugar	0g
Protein	3g

Easy Vegan French Toast

SERVES 4

Per Serving:

Calories	378
Fat	10g
Sodium	339mg
Carbohydrates	57g
Fiber	8g
Sugar	17g
Protein	13g

THE PERFECT VEGAN FRENCH TOAST

Creating an eggless French toast is a true art. Is your French toast too soggy or too dry? Thickly sliced bread lightly toasted will be more absorbent. Too mushy, or the mixture doesn't want to stick? Try spooning it onto your bread rather than dipping the bread into the mixture.

Serve this golden fried French toast with maple syrup or agave nectar. Fresh berries or orange marmalade would be wonderful as well.

2 medium bananas, peeled

½ cup unsweetened soy milk

1 tablespoon orange juice

1 tablespoon maple syrup

¾ teaspoon vanilla extract

1 tablespoon all-purpose flour

1 teaspoon ground cinnamon

½ teaspoon ground nutmeg

2 tablespoons vegetable oil

12 (1-ounce) slices whole-grain bread

1 Place bananas, soy milk, orange juice, syrup, and vanilla in a blender or food processor. Blend 2–3 minutes until smooth and creamy.

2 Transfer to a medium bowl. Whisk in flour, cinnamon, and nutmeg. Pour into a shallow bowl.

3 In a large skillet, heat oil over medium-high heat.

4 Dip bread into banana mixture and turn to coat all sides. Fry in hot oil 2–3 minutes, turning once, until lightly golden brown on both sides. Serve immediately.

Baked "Sausage" and Mushroom Frittata

Baked tofu frittatas make easy brunch or weekend breakfasts. Once you've got the technique down, it's easy to adjust the ingredients to include your favorites. This one packs a super protein punch!

2 tablespoons olive oil

½ large onion, peeled and diced

3 cloves garlic, peeled and minced

½ cup sliced mushrooms

1 (12-ounce) package vegan sausage or vegan beef crumbles

¾ teaspoon salt

¼ teaspoon ground black pepper

1 (14-ounce) package firm or extra-firm tofu, drained and pressed

1 (14-ounce) package silken tofu, drained

1 tablespoon soy sauce

2 tablespoons nutritional yeast

¼ teaspoon ground turmeric

1 medium tomato, cored and thinly sliced

SERVES 4

Per Serving:

Calories	377
Fat	19g
Sodium	1,175mg
Carbohydrates	15g
Fiber	4g
Sugar	5g
Protein	32g

1 Preheat oven to 325°F. Spray a 9" glass pie dish with nonstick cooking spray.

2 In a large skillet, heat oil over medium heat. Add onion, garlic, mushrooms, and vegan sausage. Sauté 3–4 minutes until sausage is browned and mushrooms are soft. Transfer to a large bowl. Season with salt and pepper and set aside.

3 Add firm tofu, silken tofu, soy sauce, yeast, and turmeric to a blender. Process until mixed. Add to sausage mixture and stir to combine. Pour into prepared dish. Top with tomato slices.

4 Bake 40–45 minutes until firm. Cool 5–10 minutes before serving.

Potato-Poblano Breakfast Burritos

If you like your burritos spicy, omit the ketchup and add ½ teaspoon or more hot sauce instead.

2 tablespoons olive oil

2 small Yukon Gold potatoes, diced

2 medium poblano or Anaheim chili peppers, seeded and diced

1 teaspoon chili powder

¼ teaspoon salt

⅛ teaspoon ground black pepper

1 medium tomato, cored and diced

⅔ cup vegan beef or vegan sausage crumbles

3 (8") flour tortillas, warmed

¼ cup shredded vegan Cheddar cheese

2 tablespoons ketchup

SERVES 3

Per Serving:

Calories	424
Fat	16g
Sodium	876mg
Carbohydrates	60g
Fiber	9g
Sugar	7g
Protein	13g

1 In a medium skillet, heat oil over medium heat. Add potatoes and chilies and sauté 6–7 minutes until potatoes are tender.

2 Stir in chili powder, salt, black pepper, tomato, and vegan crumbles.

3 Continue cooking another 4–5 minutes until potatoes and tomatoes are soft and crumbles are cooked.

4 Divide mixture evenly among tortillas and top with vegan cheese and ketchup. Roll tortillas up burrito-style and serve immediately.

Tofu Florentine

Satisfy your comfort food cravings with this "eggy" tofu and spinach mixture covered in a creamy sauce over an English muffin.

SERVES 2

Per Serving:

Calories	754
Fat	48g
Sodium	1,493mg
Carbohydrates	47g
Fiber	9g
Sugar	6g
Protein	31g

BENEDICT VS. FLORENTINE

For a variation on this classic brunch recipe, skip the spinach and add a layer of lightly browned vegan bacon for Tofu Benedict instead of Florentine.

2 tablespoons all-purpose flour

1 teaspoon nutritional yeast

1 teaspoon garlic powder

2 tablespoons canola or safflower oil

1 (14-ounce) package firm or extra-firm tofu, drained, pressed, and sliced into 4 slabs

1 (10-ounce) package frozen spinach, thawed and drained

½ cup Quick Hollandaise Sauce (see recipe in Chapter 2)

2 vegan English muffins, split and lightly toasted

1 In a shallow bowl, combine flour, yeast, and garlic powder.
2 In a large skillet, heat oil over medium-high heat. Dredge tofu in flour mixture and fry 2–3 minutes on each side until lightly browned.
3 Reduce heat to low and add spinach and Quick Hollandaise Sauce. Stir gently to coat tofu with sauce.
4 Cook 1–2 minutes until spinach is heated through.
5 Place 1 piece tofu on each English muffin half and spoon spinach and sauce over top. Serve immediately.

Quinoa Pudding

Instead of tapioca pudding or baked rice pudding, try this whole-grain version made with quinoa. It's healthy enough to eat for breakfast, but sweet enough for dessert.

1 cup uncooked white quinoa

2 cups water

2 cups unsweetened soy milk

2 tablespoons maple syrup or brown rice syrup

1 teaspoon cornstarch

2 medium bananas, peeled and thinly sliced

½ teaspoon vanilla extract

⅓ cup raisins

⅛ teaspoon ground cinnamon

SERVES 4

Per Serving:

Calories	339
Fat	3g
Sodium	72mg
Carbohydrates	65g
Fiber	6g
Sugar	26g
Protein	11g

1 In a medium saucepan over medium-high heat, combine quinoa and water. Bring to a boil, then reduce heat to medium-low. Cover pan and simmer, stirring frequently, 10–15 minutes until water is absorbed.

2 Stir in soy milk, syrup, cornstarch, and bananas. Cook, stirring constantly, 6–8 minutes until bananas are soft and pudding has thickened.

3 Remove from heat, stir in vanilla and raisins, and sprinkle with cinnamon.

4 Serve warm or cold.

Chocolate–Peanut Butter Breakfast Quinoa

SERVES 3

Per Serving:

Calories	256
Fat	7g
Sodium	69mg
Carbohydrates	34g
Fiber	5g
Sugar	11g
Protein	10g

QUINOA FLAKES

If you discover you like eating quinoa for breakfast, try quinoa flakes instead of whole quinoa. They cook quicker, like oatmeal, but provide the same protein and amino acids that make quinoa such a great choice for vegans.

Chocolate and peanut butter is a flavor combination from heaven. This breakfast cereal is much more nutritious than processed cereal you can buy in the store.

½ cup uncooked white quinoa

1½ cups unsweetened soy milk

2 tablespoons peanut butter

1½ tablespoons unsweetened cocoa powder

1½ tablespoons maple syrup or brown rice syrup

1 In a medium saucepan over medium-low heat, combine quinoa and soy milk. Bring to a boil, then reduce heat to medium-low. Cover pan and simmer, stirring frequently, 10–15 minutes until quinoa is tender and soy milk is absorbed.

2 Remove from heat and stir in peanut butter, cocoa powder, and syrup.

3 Serve immediately.

CHAPTER 4

Salads and Salad Dressings

Sesame and Soy Coleslaw Salad

SERVES 4

Per Serving:

Calories	180
Fat	9g
Sodium	191mg
Carbohydrates	22g
Fiber	6g
Sugar	14g
Protein	4g

You don't need mayonnaise to make a coleslaw. Dressing the salad with a vinaigrette creates a lighter version. Make it a full meal by adding some baked or pan-fried tofu.

1 small head Napa cabbage, cored and shredded

1 medium carrot, peeled and grated

2 scallions, trimmed and chopped

1 medium red bell pepper, seeded and thinly sliced

2 tablespoons olive oil

2 tablespoons apple cider vinegar

2 teaspoons soy sauce

½ teaspoon sesame oil

2 tablespoons maple syrup

2 tablespoons sesame seeds

1 In a large bowl, toss together cabbage, carrot, scallions, and bell pepper.

2 In a small bowl, whisk together olive oil, vinegar, soy sauce, sesame oil, and syrup.

3 Drizzle dressing over cabbage mixture, add sesame seeds, and toss to combine.

4 Divide among four plates and serve.

Raspberry Vinaigrette

Create a colorful and inviting salad with this vibrant dressing. Use it to dress up a fruit salad, or toss it with a sweet and savory salad made with baby spinach, dried cranberries, and toasted pine nuts.

¼ cup balsamic or raspberry vinegar

2 tablespoons lime juice

¼ cup raspberry preserves

2 tablespoons Dijon mustard

½ teaspoon sugar

¾ cup olive oil

½ teaspoon salt

¼ teaspoon ground black pepper

1 Place vinegar, lime juice, raspberry preserves, mustard, and sugar in a food processor or blender. Process 1–2 minutes until smooth.

2 While blender is running on high speed, slowly add olive oil a few drops at a time to allow oil to emulsify. Season with salt and pepper.

3 Serve immediately or refrigerate covered up to 2 weeks.

MAKES 1¼ CUPS

Per Serving (2 tablespoons):

Calories	178
Fat	16g
Sodium	195mg
Carbohydrates	7g
Fiber	0g
Sugar	5g
Protein	0g

Dairy-Free Ranch Dressing

MAKES 1 CUP

Per Serving (2 tablespoons):

Calories	120
Fat	10g
Sodium	262mg
Carbohydrates	3g
Fiber	0g
Sugar	1g
Protein	4g

This versatile dressing is good drizzled on salads, but it's also a wonderful dip for anything from baby carrots to French fries or even pizza.

1 cup Vegan Mayonnaise (see recipe in Chapter 2)

¼ cup unsweetened soy milk

1 teaspoon Dijon mustard

1 tablespoon lemon juice

1 teaspoon onion powder

¾ teaspoon garlic powder

1 tablespoon minced fresh chives

1 In a medium bowl, combine Vegan Mayonnaise, soy milk, mustard, lemon juice, onion powder, and garlic powder. Whisk 30 seconds until smooth.

2 Stir in chives. Serve immediately or refrigerate covered up to 1 week.

Creamy Miso-Sesame Dressing

A bit of minced fresh ginger would add another layer of flavor to this creamy and tangy Japanese-inspired salad dressing if you happen to have some on hand.

¼ cup miso
2 tablespoons rice vinegar
¼ cup soy sauce
2 tablespoons sesame oil
½ cup unsweetened soy milk
2 tablespoons lime juice

1 Place all ingredients in a blender or food processor and process 1–2 minutes until smooth.
2 Serve immediately or refrigerate covered up to 2 weeks.

MAKES 1 CUP

Per Serving (2 tablespoons):

Calories	56
Fat	4g
Sodium	798mg
Carbohydrates	3g
Fiber	1g
Sugar	2g
Protein	2g

MISO

Miso is available in a variety of interchangeable flavors and colors; red, white, and barley miso are the most common. It's really a personal preference which type you use. Asian grocers stock miso at about one-third the price of other merchants, so if you're lucky enough to have one in your neighborhood, it's worth a trip.

Messy Taco Salad

SERVES 4

Per Serving:

Calories	365
Fat	20g
Sodium	1,105mg
Carbohydrates	38g
Fiber	10g
Sugar	9g
Protein	9g

BAKED TORTILLA CHIPS

Make your own tortilla chips: Slice whole-wheat tortillas into strips or triangles and arrange in a single layer on a large baking sheet. Drizzle or spray with olive oil and season with a bit of salt and garlic powder, or just bake them plain. It'll take 5–6 minutes on each side in a 300°F oven.

If you're bored with the usual salads but still want something light and green, try this taco salad. It's best made with iceberg lettuce, but if you want something more nutritious, use a blend of half iceberg and half romaine. Drizzle with a little hot sauce if you'd like.

2 medium heads iceberg lettuce, cored and chopped

½ cup sliced black olives

½ cup corn kernels

1 small jalapeño pepper, seeded and sliced

1 (15-ounce) can vegan refried black beans

2 tablespoons taco sauce

¼ cup bottled salsa

¼ cup vegan mayonnaise

12 tortilla chips, crumbled

1 medium avocado, peeled, pitted, and diced

¾ cup shredded vegan Cheddar cheese

1 In a large bowl, combine lettuce, olives, corn, and jalapeño.
2 Place refried beans in a small microwave-safe bowl and microwave on high 1 minute. Stir in taco sauce, salsa, and mayonnaise, breaking up beans and mixing to form a thick sauce.
3 Combine bean mixture with lettuce mixture, stirring to combine as much as possible. Add tortilla chips and avocado and stir gently to combine.
4 Sprinkle with vegan Cheddar and serve.

Thai Orange-Peanut Dressing

MAKES ¾ CUP

Per Serving (2 tablespoons):

Calories	75
Fat	5g
Sodium	294mg
Carbohydrates	4g
Fiber	1g
Sugar	2g
Protein	3g

This dressing is a sweet and spicy take on traditional peanut satay sauce. Serve it over salad or add a bit less orange juice to use it as a dip for vegetables.

¼ **cup peanut butter**

¼ **cup orange juice**

2 **tablespoons soy sauce**

2 **tablespoons rice vinegar**

2 **tablespoons water**

½ **teaspoon garlic powder**

½ **teaspoon sugar**

¼ **teaspoon crushed red pepper flakes**

1   In a medium bowl, whisk together all ingredients 30 seconds until smooth and creamy, adding more or less liquid to achieve desired consistency.

2   Serve immediately or refrigerate covered up to 2 weeks.

Kidney Bean and Chickpea Salad

This marinated two-bean salad is perfect for summer picnics or as a side dish for barbecues and potlucks.

¼ cup olive oil

¼ cup red wine vinegar

½ teaspoon paprika

2 tablespoons lemon juice

1 (15-ounce) can chickpeas, drained and rinsed

1 (15-ounce) can kidney beans, drained and rinsed

½ cup sliced black olives

1 (8-ounce) can corn kernels, drained

½ medium red onion, peeled and chopped

1 tablespoon chopped fresh parsley

½ teaspoon salt

½ teaspoon ground black pepper

SERVES 6

Per Serving:

Calories	252
Fat	12g
Sodium	545mg
Carbohydrates	27g
Fiber	7g
Sugar	3g
Protein	8g

1 In a medium bowl, whisk together oil, vinegar, paprika, and lemon juice.

2 In a large bowl, combine chickpeas, kidney beans, olives, corn, onion, and parsley. Pour olive oil mixture over bean mixture and toss to combine. Season with salt and pepper.

3 Cover and refrigerate at least 1 hour before serving.

Warm German Potato Salad

Per Serving:

Calories	362
Fat	8g
Sodium	498mg
Carbohydrates	63g
Fiber	8g
Sugar	5g
Protein	9g

Tangy deli-style German potato salad requires potatoes that are thinly sliced and not overcooked. This vegan version is just as good—if not better—than any other recipe you'll find.

6 medium Yukon Gold potatoes

2 tablespoons olive oil

1 small onion, peeled and thinly sliced

⅓ cup distilled white vinegar or apple cider vinegar

1 tablespoon Dijon mustard

1 tablespoon all-purpose flour

1 teaspoon sugar

⅓ cup water

2 medium scallions, trimmed and chopped

3 tablespoons vegan bacon bits

½ teaspoon salt

½ teaspoon ground black pepper

1 Fill a large saucepan with water and bring to a boil over high heat. Add potatoes, cover pan, and reduce heat to medium. Cook about 20 minutes until potatoes are tender when pierced with a knife. Drain and set aside to cool 30 minutes. Slice cooled potatoes into thin rounds, place in a large bowl, and set aside.

2 Heat oil in a large skillet over medium heat. Add onion and sauté 2–3 minutes until just barely soft.

3 Add vinegar, mustard, flour, sugar, and water, stirring to combine. Bring to a simmer, reduce heat to low, and cook 1–2 minutes until thickened. Remove from heat and pour over potatoes. Stir in scallions, vegan bacon bits, salt, and pepper.

4 Serve warm or at room temperature.

Balsamic Vinaigrette

There's no need to buy expensive, sugar-laden salad dressings at the grocery store. It takes less than a minute to whisk together a superior dressing at home.

¼ cup balsamic vinegar

¾ cup olive oil

1 tablespoon Dijon mustard

¼ teaspoon salt

⅛ teaspoon ground black pepper

½ teaspoon dried basil

½ teaspoon dried parsley

1 In a small bowl, whisk together all ingredients 30 seconds until well combined.

2 Serve immediately or refrigerate covered up to 2 weeks.

MAKES 1 CUP

Per Serving (2 tablespoons):

Calories	189
Fat	20g
Sodium	121mg
Carbohydrates	2g
Fiber	0g
Sugar	1g
Protein	0g

Italian White Bean and Herb Salad

SERVES 4

Per Serving:

Calories	292
Fat	13g
Sodium	957mg
Carbohydrates	39g
Fiber	15g
Sugar	4g
Protein	12g

Don't let the simplicity of this bean salad fool you! The fresh herbs flavor the beans to perfection, so there's no need to add anything else.

3 tablespoons olive oil

2 (15-ounce) cans cannellini or great northern beans, drained and rinsed

2 stalks celery, diced

¼ cup chopped fresh parsley

¼ cup chopped fresh basil

3 large tomatoes, cored and chopped

½ cup sliced black olives

2 tablespoons lemon juice

½ teaspoon salt

¼ teaspoon ground black pepper

¼ teaspoon crushed red pepper flakes

1 In a large skillet, heat oil over medium-low heat. Add beans, celery, parsley, and basil. Cook, stirring frequently, 3 minutes until herbs are softened but not cooked.

2 Remove from heat and stir in tomatoes, olives, lemon juice, salt, black pepper, and red pepper flakes. Toss to combine.

3 Refrigerate at least 1 hour before serving.

Spicy-Sweet Cucumber Salad

Japanese cucumber salad is cool and refreshing but has a bit of spice. Enjoy it as a healthy afternoon snack or as a fresh accompaniment to a takeout dinner.

2 medium cucumbers, thinly sliced

¾ teaspoon salt

½ small onion, peeled and thinly sliced

¼ cup rice vinegar

1 tablespoon agave nectar

1 teaspoon sesame oil

¼ teaspoon crushed red pepper flakes

SERVES 2

Per Serving:

Calories	99
Fat	2g
Sodium	661mg
Carbohydrates	18g
Fiber	2g
Sugar	11g
Protein	2g

1 In a large shallow container or baking sheet, spread cucumber slices in a single layer and sprinkle with salt. Set aside at least 10 minutes.

2 Drain cucumber slices and place in a medium bowl. Add onion slices.

3 In a small bowl, whisk together vinegar, agave, oil, and red pepper flakes. Pour dressing over cucumber mixture and toss gently.

4 Set aside at least 10 minutes before serving.

Tangerine and Mint Salad

Fennel, mint, and tangerines make a wonderful combination. A small drizzle of flavored oil, if you have some, would kick up the flavor even more. Try walnut or truffle oil.

1 medium head Boston lettuce, cored and chopped

2 tablespoons chopped fresh mint

2 medium tangerines or clementines, peeled and sectioned

⅓ cup chopped walnuts

1 medium bulb fennel, trimmed and thinly sliced

2 tablespoons olive oil

¼ teaspoon salt

⅛ teaspoon ground black pepper

1 In a large bowl, gently toss lettuce, mint, tangerines, walnuts, and fennel together.

2 Drizzle with olive oil, salt, and pepper.

3 Divide between two plates and serve.

SERVES 2

Per Serving:

Calories	340
Fat	26g
Sodium	356mg
Carbohydrates	25g
Fiber	8g
Sugar	15g
Protein	6g

HOMEMADE FLAVORED OILS

A flavored oil will beautify your kitchen and add flavor to your food. Simply combine several of your favorite herbs, whole garlic cloves, peppercorns, dried lemon or orange zest, or dried chilies with a quality olive oil. For safety's sake, avoid fresh herbs and zests, and always use dried. Oils infused with dried herbs will keep up to one year, while fresh herbs can spoil after less than a week.

Edamame Salad

SERVES 4

Per Serving:

Calories	226
Fat	14g
Sodium	403mg
Carbohydrates	16g
Fiber	8g
Sugar	4g
Protein	11g

CONVENIENT EDAMAME

Edamame, or baby green soybeans, are a great source of unprocessed soy protein. You're probably familiar with the lightly steamed and salted edamame served as an appetizer at Japanese restaurants, but many grocers sell shelled edamame in the frozen foods section.

If you can't find shelled edamame, try this recipe with lima beans instead.

2 cups frozen shelled edamame, thawed and drained

1 medium red or yellow bell pepper, seeded and diced

¾ cup corn kernels

3 tablespoons chopped fresh cilantro

3 tablespoons olive oil

2 tablespoons red wine vinegar

1 teaspoon soy sauce

1 teaspoon chili powder

2 teaspoons lemon juice

½ teaspoon salt

½ teaspoon ground black pepper

1 In a large bowl, combine edamame, bell pepper, corn, and cilantro.

2 In a small bowl, whisk together oil, vinegar, soy sauce, chili powder, lemon juice, salt, and black pepper. Pour over edamame mixture and toss to coat.

3 Refrigerate at least 1 hour before serving.

Spiced Couscous Salad with Bell Pepper and Zucchini

This dish can be a full meal for lunch or dinner, or a side salad, depending on how hungry you are.

2 cups vegetable broth

2 cups uncooked couscous

1 teaspoon ground cumin

½ teaspoon ground turmeric

½ teaspoon paprika

¼ teaspoon ground cayenne pepper

1 tablespoon lemon juice

2 tablespoons olive oil

2 medium zucchini, trimmed and sliced

1 large red bell pepper, seeded and chopped

1 large yellow bell pepper, seeded and chopped

3 cloves garlic, peeled and minced

2 tablespoons chopped fresh parsley

½ teaspoon salt

¼ teaspoon ground black pepper

1 In a medium saucepan over high heat, combine broth and couscous. Bring to a boil. Remove from heat and stir in cumin, turmeric, paprika, and cayenne pepper.

2 Cover saucepan and set aside 5 minutes until couscous is soft and liquid is absorbed. Fluff couscous with a fork and stir in lemon juice.

3 In a large skillet, heat oil over medium heat. Add zucchini, bell peppers, and garlic. Sauté about 5 minutes just until soft. Transfer to a large bowl and add couscous.

4 Stir in parsley, salt, and black pepper. Serve immediately.

SERVES 8	
Per Serving:	
Calories	233
Fat	4g
Sodium	359mg
Carbohydrates	42g
Fiber	4g
Sugar	3g
Protein	7g

Pineapple and Mint Rice Salad

SERVES 6

Per Serving:

Calories	308
Fat	11g
Sodium	13mg
Carbohydrates	47g
Fiber	2g
Sugar	7g
Protein	4g

Pineapple and mint are a cooling combination, so this salad is perfect for a hot day.

4 cups cooked white rice

2 stalks celery, diced

1 cup fresh or drained canned diced pineapple

⅓ cup chopped macadamia nuts or cashews

¼ cup dried papaya pieces

⅓ cup pineapple juice

2 tablespoons olive oil

2 tablespoons red wine vinegar

¼ cup unsweetened toasted coconut flakes

2 tablespoons chopped fresh mint

1 In a large bowl, combine rice, celery, pineapple, macadamias, and papaya. Stir to mix well.

2 In a small bowl, whisk together pineapple juice, oil, and vinegar. Pour over rice mixture and toss to coat. Refrigerate at least 1 hour.

3 Gently stir in coconut flakes and mint just before serving.

Lemon-Quinoa Vegetable Salad

If you prefer to use fresh vegetables, any kind will do. Steamed broccoli or fresh tomatoes would work well.

4 cups vegetable broth

1½ cups uncooked white or red quinoa

1 (10-ounce) bag frozen mixed vegetables (peas, corn, carrots, and green beans), thawed

¼ cup lemon juice

¼ cup olive oil

1 teaspoon garlic powder

½ teaspoon salt

¼ teaspoon ground black pepper

2 tablespoons chopped fresh cilantro

SERVES 4

Per Serving:

Calories	420
Fat	17g
Sodium	1,127mg
Carbohydrates	54g
Fiber	7g
Sugar	2g
Protein	12g

1 In a large saucepan over high heat, bring broth to a boil. Add quinoa, reduce heat to low, and cover. Simmer 15 20 minutes, stirring occasionally, until liquid is absorbed and quinoa is cooked. Add mixed vegetables and stir to combine.

2 Remove from heat and stir in lemon juice, oil, garlic powder, salt, pepper, and cilantro. Serve hot or cold.

Spinach Salad with Strawberries and Beets

SERVES 4

Per Serving:

Calories	287
Fat	23g
Sodium	367mg
Carbohydrates	19g
Fiber	5g
Sugar	12g
Protein	4g

Colorful and nutritious, this vibrant red salad can be made with roasted or canned beets, or even raw grated beets if you prefer.

3 small beets, peeled, trimmed, and chopped

5 ounces baby spinach

1 cup sliced strawberries

½ cup chopped pecans

¼ cup olive oil

2 tablespoons red wine vinegar

2 tablespoons agave nectar

2 tablespoons orange juice

½ teaspoon salt

¼ teaspoon ground black pepper

1 In a small saucepan over medium-high heat, place beets and cover with water. Bring to a boil. Boil until tender, about 15 minutes. Drain and set aside to cool at least 30 minutes.

2 In a large bowl, combine spinach, strawberries, pecans, and cooled beets.

3 In a small bowl, whisk together oil, vinegar, agave, and orange juice. Pour over salad and toss to coat.

4 Season with salt and pepper and serve.

Tabbouleh Salad with Chickpeas

SERVES 4

Per Serving:

Calories	339
Fat	12g
Sodium	450mg
Carbohydrates	51g
Fiber	11g
Sugar	7g
Protein	11g

TABBOULEH SANDWICHES

Spread a slice of bread or a tortilla with some hummus, then layer tabbouleh, sweet pickle relish, thinly sliced cucumbers, and some lettuce to make a quick sandwich or wrap for lunch.

Though you'll need to adjust the cooking time, of course, you can try this tabbouleh recipe with just about any whole grain. Bulgur wheat is traditional, but quinoa, millet, or amaranth would also work.

1 cup bulgur wheat

1¼ cups boiling water

3 tablespoons olive oil

¼ cup lemon juice

1 teaspoon garlic powder

½ teaspoon salt

½ teaspoon ground black pepper

3 scallions, trimmed and chopped

½ cup chopped fresh mint

½ cup chopped fresh parsley

1 (15-ounce) can chickpeas, drained and rinsed

3 large tomatoes, cored and diced

1 In a large bowl, add bulgur and pour boiling water over bulgur. Cover and set aside 30 minutes until bulgur is soft. Transfer to a medium bowl.

2 In a small bowl, whisk together oil, lemon juice, garlic powder, salt, and pepper. Pour over bulgur and stir to combine.

3 Stir in scallions, mint, parsley, and chickpeas. Carefully fold in tomatoes.

4 Refrigerate at least 1 hour before serving.

Black Bean and Barley Taco Salad

Adding barley to a taco salad gives a nutritious whole-grain and fiber boost to this low-fat recipe.

1 (15-ounce) can black beans, drained and rinsed

½ teaspoon ground cumin

½ teaspoon dried oregano

2 tablespoons lime juice

1 teaspoon hot sauce

1 cup cooked barley

1 medium head iceberg lettuce, cored and shredded

¾ cup bottled salsa

4 large tortilla chips, crumbled

2 tablespoons vegan Italian dressing

SERVES 2

Per Serving:

Calories	331
Fat	4g
Sodium	1,441mg
Carbohydrates	76g
Fiber	24g
Sugar	14g
Protein	17g

1 In a large bowl, combine beans, cumin, oregano, lime juice, and hot sauce. Mash together until beans are slightly chunky. Stir in barley.
2 Spread lettuce on a large plate or platter. Layer with bean mixture, salsa, and tortilla chips. Drizzle with Italian dressing and serve.

CHAPTER 5

Soups

Ten-Minute Chili

No time? No problem! This is a quick and easy way to get dinner on the table. Instead of veggie burgers, you could toss in a handful of TVP flakes or any other mock meat you happen to have on hand.

SERVES 4

Per Serving:

Calories	402
Fat	6g
Sodium	1,632mg
Carbohydrates	61g
Fiber	23g
Sugar	9g
Protein	26g

1 (12-ounce) jar salsa

1 (14.5-ounce) can diced tomatoes

2 (15-ounce) cans kidney beans, drained and rinsed

1 (10-ounce) bag frozen mixed vegetables (peas, corn, carrots, and green beans), thawed

4 frozen veggie burgers, thawed and crumbled

2 tablespoons chili powder

1 teaspoon ground cumin

½ cup water

1 In a stockpot or Dutch oven, combine all ingredients together. Bring to a boil over high heat. Reduce heat to medium-low, cover, and simmer 10 minutes, stirring frequently.

2 Serve immediately.

Cashew Cream of Asparagus Soup

This dairy-free soup uses a rich cashew base to bring out the natural flavors of the asparagus.

2 tablespoons olive oil

1 medium onion, peeled and chopped

4 cloves garlic, peeled and minced

2 pounds asparagus, trimmed and chopped

4 cups vegetable broth

¾ cup raw cashews

¾ cup water

¼ teaspoon ground sage

½ teaspoon salt

¼ teaspoon ground black pepper

2 teaspoons lemon juice

2 tablespoons nutritional yeast

1 In a stockpot or Dutch oven, heat oil over medium-high heat. Add onion and garlic and sauté 4–5 minutes until onion is soft. Stir in asparagus and broth. Bring to a boil.

2 Reduce heat to medium-low, cover, and simmer 20 minutes. Remove from heat and let sit 10 minutes until slightly cooled. Transfer soup to a blender in batches and purée until almost smooth. Return mixture to stockpot over low heat.

3 Place cashews and water in a food processor or blender and purée until smooth. Add to soup with sage, salt, and pepper and heat 2 more minutes, stirring to combine.

4 Stir in lemon juice and yeast just before serving.

SERVES 4

Per Serving:

Calories	287
Fat	19g
Sodium	1,101mg
Carbohydrates	21g
Fiber	5g
Sugar	7g
Protein	10g

VARIETIES OF VEGETABLE BROTHS

A basic vegetable broth is made by simmering vegetables and a bay leaf or two in water for at least 30 minutes. While you may be familiar with the canned and boxed stocks available at the grocery store, vegan chefs have a few other tricks up their sleeves to impart extra flavor to recipes calling for vegetable broth. Check your natural grocer for specialty flavored bouillon cubes such as vegan "chicken" or "beef" flavor, or shop the bulk bins for powdered vegetable broth mix.

Tom Kha Kai

In Thailand, this soup is a full meal, served alongside a large plate of steamed rice. The vegetables vary with the season and whim of the chef—broccoli, bell peppers, or mild chilies are common. Don't worry if you can't find lemongrass or galangal—use lime zest and grated ginger instead.

1 (14-ounce) can coconut milk

2 cups vegetable broth

1 tablespoon soy sauce

3 cloves garlic, peeled and minced

5 (¼") slices fresh peeled galangal or ginger

1 stalk lemongrass, chopped

1 tablespoon lime juice

2 small Thai chili peppers, seeded and sliced

½ teaspoon crushed red pepper flakes

1 medium onion, peeled and chopped

2 medium tomatoes, cored and chopped

1 large carrot, peeled and thinly sliced

½ cup sliced mushrooms

¼ cup chopped fresh cilantro

SERVES 4

Per Serving:

Calories	254
Fat	20g
Sodium	652mg
Carbohydrates	16g
Fiber	2g
Sugar	6g
Protein	4g

1 In a large saucepan over medium-low heat, combine coconut milk and broth. Add soy sauce, garlic, galangal, lemongrass, lime juice, chilies, and red pepper flakes. Heat about 10 minutes until hot, but do not boil.

2 Add onion, tomatoes, carrot, and mushrooms. Reduce heat to low, cover, and simmer 10 minutes.

3 Remove from heat. Top with cilantro before serving.

Shiitake and Garlic Broth

Shiitake mushrooms make a rich stock with a deep flavor.

MAKES 6 CUPS

Per Serving (1 cup):

Calories	4
Fat	0g
Sodium	0mg
Carbohydrates	1g
Fiber	0g
Sugar	0g
Protein	0g

VEGAN DASHI

To turn this into a Japanese dashi stock for miso and noodle soups, omit the bay leaf and thyme and add a generous amount of seaweed, preferably kombu, if you can find it.

⅓ cup dried shiitake mushrooms

6 cups water

2 cloves garlic, peeled and crushed

1 bay leaf

½ teaspoon dried thyme

1 small onion, peeled and chopped

1 In a stockpot or Dutch oven over high heat, combine all ingredients. Bring to a boil.

2 Reduce heat to low, cover, and simmer 40 minutes.

3 Strain before using.

Cream of Carrot Soup with Coconut

The addition of coconut milk transforms an ordinary carrot and ginger soup into an unexpected treat.

3 medium carrots, peeled and chopped

1 large sweet potato, peeled and chopped

1 medium onion, peeled and chopped

3½ cups vegetable broth

3 cloves garlic, peeled and minced

2 teaspoons minced fresh ginger

1 (14-ounce) can coconut milk

1 teaspoon salt

¾ teaspoon ground cinnamon

SERVES 6	
Per Serving:	
Calories	178
Fat	13g
Sodium	891mg
Carbohydrates	13g
Fiber	2g
Sugar	5g
Protein	2g

1 In a stockpot or Dutch oven over high heat, combine carrots, sweet potato, onion, broth, garlic, and ginger. Bring to a boil over high heat. Reduce heat to medium-low, cover, and simmer 20–25 minutes until carrots and sweet potato are soft.

2 Remove from heat and let sit 5 minutes until slightly cooled. Transfer soup to a blender in batches and purée until smooth.

3 Return soup to pot. Over very low heat, stir in coconut milk and salt. Heat another 3–4 minutes just until warmed through.

4 Sprinkle with cinnamon just before serving.

White Bean and Corn Chowder

SERVES 4

Per Serving:

Calories	268
Fat	7g
Sodium	911mg
Carbohydrates	42g
Fiber	9g
Sugar	9g
Protein	11g

FRESH IS ALWAYS BEST

Cans are convenient, but dried beans are cheaper, need less packaging, and add a better flavor. And if you plan in advance, they aren't much work at all to prepare. Place beans in a large pot, cover with water (more than you think you'll need), and set aside at least 2 hours or overnight. Drain the water and simmer in fresh water about an hour, then you're good to go! One cup dried beans yields about 3 cups cooked.

This is a filling and satisfying soup that could easily be a main dish. Add chopped collard greens and a dash of hot sauce for more nutrition and spice.

2 tablespoons olive oil

1 medium red potato, peeled and chopped

1 medium onion, peeled and chopped

3 cups vegetable broth

1½ cups corn kernels

1 (15-ounce) can cannellini beans, drained and rinsed

½ teaspoon dried thyme

¼ teaspoon ground black pepper

1 tablespoon all-purpose flour

1½ cups unsweetened soy milk

1 In a stockpot or Dutch oven, heat oil over medium-high heat. Add potato and onion and sauté 5 minutes. Add broth and bring to a boil.

2 Reduce heat to medium-low, cover, and simmer 15 minutes.

3 Stir in corn, beans, thyme, and pepper.

4 In a small bowl, whisk together flour and soy milk, then add to the pot, stirring well to prevent lumps. Cook uncovered 5–6 more minutes, stirring frequently, until thickened.

5 Cool 5 minutes before serving.

Barley-Vegetable Soup

Barley-Vegetable Soup is an excellent "kitchen sink" recipe—you can toss in just about any fresh or frozen vegetables you happen to have on hand.

2 tablespoons olive oil

1 medium onion, peeled and chopped

2 large carrots, peeled and sliced

2 stalks celery, chopped

8 cups vegetable broth

1 cup uncooked barley

1 (10-ounce) bag frozen mixed vegetables (peas, corn, carrots, and green beans), thawed

1 (14.5-ounce) can diced tomatoes

½ teaspoon dried parsley

½ teaspoon dried thyme

2 bay leaves

½ teaspoon salt

½ teaspoon ground black pepper

SERVES 6

Per Serving:

Calories	155
Fat	5g
Sodium	1,435mg
Carbohydrates	24g
Fiber	5g
Sugar	7g
Protein	3g

1 In a stockpot or Dutch oven, heat oil over medium-high heat. Add onion, carrots, and celery. Sauté 3–5 minutes until onion is almost soft.

2 Add broth, barley, mixed vegetables, tomatoes, parsley, thyme, and bay leaves. Bring to a boil. Reduce heat to medium-low, cover, and simmer 45 minutes, stirring occasionally. Remove cover and simmer 10 more minutes.

3 Remove and discard bay leaves; season with salt and pepper. Serve immediately.

Gazpacho with Avocado

CRUNCHY CROUTONS

Slice your favorite vegan artisan bread, focaccia, or whatever you've got into 1" cubes. Toss them in a large bowl with a generous coating of olive oil or a flavored oil, a bit of salt, Italian seasoning, garlic powder, and a dash of ground cayenne pepper. Transfer to a baking sheet and bake at 275°F 15–20 minutes until crisp, tossing once or twice. Use them right away or keep them in an airtight container up to 1 week.

This soup is best enjoyed on an outdoor patio just after sunset on a warm summer evening. But really, anytime you want a simple, light starter soup will do, no matter the weather. Add some crunch by topping with homemade croutons.

2 medium cucumbers, peeled and diced

½ small red onion, peeled and diced

2 large tomatoes, cored and diced

¼ cup chopped fresh cilantro

2 medium avocados, peeled, pitted, and diced

4 cloves garlic, peeled

2 tablespoons lime juice

1 tablespoon red wine vinegar

¾ cup vegetable broth

1 small jalapeño or serrano pepper, trimmed and seeded

½ teaspoon salt

½ teaspoon ground black pepper

1 In a large bowl, mix together cucumbers, onion, tomatoes, cilantro, and avocados. Place half of the mixture in a blender or food processor and set aside the other half. Add garlic, lime juice, vinegar, broth, and jalapeño to the blender and process until smooth.

2 Transfer purée to a serving bowl and add reserved cucumber mixture, stirring gently to combine. Season with salt and black pepper.

3 Refrigerate at least 2 hours before serving.

Easy Roasted Tomato Soup

SERVES 4

Per Serving:

Calories	152
Fat	7g
Sodium	487mg
Carbohydrates	16g
Fiber	4g
Sugar	10g
Protein	5g

Use the freshest, ripest, juiciest red tomatoes you can find for this supereasy recipe. If you need a bit more spice, add a spoonful of nutritional yeast, a dash of ground cayenne pepper, or an extra shake of salt and pepper.

6 large tomatoes, cored and sliced in half

1 small onion, peeled and quartered

4 cloves garlic, peeled

2 tablespoons olive oil

1¼ cups unsweetened soy milk

2 tablespoons chopped fresh basil

1½ teaspoons balsamic vinegar

¾ teaspoon salt

¼ teaspoon ground black pepper

1 Preheat oven to 425°F.
2 Place tomatoes, onion, and garlic on a large baking sheet and drizzle with olive oil.
3 Roast 45 minutes to 1 hour until vegetables are soft.
4 Carefully transfer roasted vegetables to a blender or food processor, including any juices on the baking sheet. Add soy milk, basil, vinegar, salt, and pepper and purée until almost smooth.
5 Transfer to a large saucepan over low heat. Cook 5 minutes until warmed through.
6 Serve immediately.

Udon Noodle Buddha Bowls

This is a nutritious full meal in a bowl, which might be particularly comforting when you're on the edge of a cold. For an authentic Japanese flavor, add a large piece of kombu seaweed to the broth or use a vegan dashi stock.

2 (8-ounce) packages uncooked udon noodles

3½ cups Shiitake and Garlic Broth (see recipe in this chapter)

1½ teaspoons minced fresh ginger

1 tablespoon sugar

1 tablespoon soy sauce

1 tablespoon rice vinegar

¼ teaspoon crushed red pepper flakes

1 medium head baby bok choy, cored and sliced

1 cup sliced fresh mushrooms

1 (14-ounce) package silken tofu, drained and cubed

¼ cup bean sprouts

1 cup chopped fresh spinach

1 teaspoon sesame oil

1 Fill a large pot with water and bring to a boil over high heat. Add noodles and cook about 5 minutes until soft. Drain noodles and divide among four serving bowls. Set aside.

2 In a large saucepan over medium-high heat, combine broth, ginger, sugar, soy sauce, vinegar, and red pepper flakes. Bring to a boil. Reduce heat to medium-low and add bok choy, mushrooms, and tofu. Simmer about 10 minutes until vegetables are soft.

3 Add bean sprouts and spinach and simmer 1 more minute until spinach has wilted.

4 Remove from heat and drizzle with sesame oil.

5 Ladle soup into the four bowls containing cooked noodles and serve immediately.

SERVES 4

Per Serving:

Calories	508
Fat	6g
Sodium	1,096mg
Carbohydrates	96g
Fiber	5g
Sugar	7g
Protein	21g

KNOW YOUR NOODLES: UDON, SOMEN, SOBA, SHIRATAKI

Udon noodles have a thick and chewy texture, but you can try this recipe with any noodle you like. Asian noodles cook quicker than pasta, so they're great when you're super hungry or in a hurry. Many grocery stores stock shirataki noodles—a high-protein, low-carb noodle that doesn't need to be cooked—perfect for hungry vegans to slurp! Check the refrigerated section for these.

Winter Seitan Stew

SERVES 6

Per Serving:

Calories	277
Fat	5g
Sodium	1,081mg
Carbohydrates	37g
Fiber	4g
Sugar	6g
Protein	22g

If you're used to a "meat and potatoes" kind of diet, this hearty seitan and potato stew will become a favorite.

2 tablespoons olive oil

2 cups chopped seitan

1 medium onion, peeled and chopped

2 large carrots, peeled and chopped

2 stalks celery, chopped

4 cups vegetable broth

2 large Yukon Gold potatoes, peeled and chopped

½ teaspoon ground sage

½ teaspoon dried rosemary

½ teaspoon dried thyme

2 tablespoons cornstarch

⅓ cup water

¼ teaspoon salt

¼ teaspoon ground black pepper

1 In a stockpot or Dutch oven, heat oil over medium-high heat. Add seitan, onion, carrots, and celery. Sauté 4–5 minutes, stirring frequently, until seitan is lightly browned.

2 Add broth and potatoes and bring to a boil. Reduce heat to low and stir in sage, rosemary, and thyme. Cover and simmer 25–30 minutes until potatoes are soft.

3 In a small bowl, whisk together cornstarch and water. Add to soup, stirring to combine.

4 Cook uncovered another 5–7 minutes until stew has thickened.

5 Season with salt and pepper and serve.

African Peanut Soup with Spinach

Cut back on the red pepper flakes to make this soup for kids, or reduce the liquids to turn it into a thick and chunky curry to pour over rice. Although the ingredients are all familiar, this is definitely not a boring meal!

2 tablespoons olive oil

1 large onion, peeled and diced

3 large tomatoes, cored and chopped

2 cups vegetable broth

1 cup canned coconut milk

⅓ cup peanut butter

1 (15-ounce) can chickpeas, drained and rinsed

½ teaspoon salt

1 teaspoon curry powder

1 teaspoon sugar

¼ teaspoon crushed red pepper flakes

5 ounces baby spinach

1 In a stockpot or Dutch oven, heat oil over medium-high heat. Add onion and tomatoes and sauté 4–5 minutes until onion is soft.

2 Add broth, coconut milk, peanut butter, chickpeas, salt, curry powder, sugar, and red pepper flakes, stirring well to combine. Bring to a boil.

3 Reduce heat to medium-low and simmer uncovered 10 minutes, stirring occasionally.

4 Stir in spinach and cook another 2 minutes until spinach is wilted.

5 Serve hot.

SERVES 4

Per Serving:

Calories	445
Fat	30g
Sodium	872mg
Carbohydrates	33g
Fiber	8g
Sugar	12g
Protein	13g

"Chicken" Noodle Soup

SERVES 6

Per Serving:

Calories	100
Fat	0g
Sodium	918mg
Carbohydrates	18g
Fiber	3g
Sugar	5g
Protein	6g

If you're sick in bed, this brothy soup is just as comforting and nutritious as the real thing.

6 cups vegetable broth

1 large carrot, peeled and diced

2 stalks celery, diced

1 large onion, peeled and chopped

½ cup minced TVP

2 bay leaves

1½ teaspoons Italian seasoning

¼ teaspoon salt

¼ teaspoon ground black pepper

1 cup uncooked small pasta shells

1 In a stockpot or Dutch oven over medium-high heat, combine all ingredients. Bring to a boil. Reduce heat to medium-low, cover, and simmer 15–20 minutes until pasta is tender.

2 Remove bay leaves, then serve hot.

Curried Pumpkin Soup

You don't have to wait for fall to make this pumpkin soup, as canned pumpkin purée will work just fine. It's also excellent with coconut milk instead of soy milk.

2 tablespoons vegan margarine

1 medium onion, peeled and diced

3 cloves garlic, peeled and minced

1 (15-ounce) can pumpkin

3 cups vegetable broth

2 bay leaves

1 tablespoon curry powder

1 teaspoon ground cumin

½ teaspoon ground ginger

¼ teaspoon salt

1 cup unsweetened soy milk

1 Melt margarine in a stockpot or Dutch oven over medium heat. Add onion and garlic and sauté 4–5 minutes until onion is soft.

2 Add pumpkin, broth, bay leaves, curry powder, cumin, ginger, and salt. Stir to combine. Bring to a low boil.

3 Reduce heat to low, cover, and simmer 15 minutes.

4 Stir in soy milk and simmer 1–2 minutes until heated through.

5 Remove and discard bay leaves before serving.

SERVES 4

Per Serving:

Calories	113
Fat	3g
Sodium	824mg
Carbohydrates	17g
Fiber	5g
Sugar	8g
Protein	4g

DITCH THE CAN

If you've got the time, there's nothing like fresh roasted pumpkin! Make your own purée to substitute for canned. Carefully chop a medium sugar pumpkin in half, remove the seeds (save and toast those later), and roast 45 minutes to an hour in a 375°F oven. Cool, then peel off the skin and mash or purée until smooth. Whatever you don't use will keep in the freezer for next time.

White Bean and Orzo Minestrone

Italian minestrone is a simple and universally loved soup. This version uses tiny orzo pasta, cannellini beans, and plenty of vegetables.

2 tablespoons olive oil

3 cloves garlic, peeled and minced

1 medium onion, peeled and chopped

2 stalks celery, chopped

5 cups vegetable broth

1 medium carrot, peeled and diced

1 cup chopped green beans

2 small red potatoes, peeled and diced

2 medium tomatoes, cored and chopped

1 (15-ounce) can cannellini beans, drained and rinsed

1 teaspoon dried basil

½ teaspoon dried oregano

¾ cup uncooked orzo

½ teaspoon salt

½ teaspoon ground black pepper

SERVES 6

Per Serving:

Calories	301
Fat	6g
Sodium	823mg
Carbohydrates	55g
Fiber	8g
Sugar	8g
Protein	9g

1 Heat oil in a stockpot or Dutch oven over medium heat. Add garlic, onion, and celery. Sauté 3–4 minutes just until soft.

2 Stir in broth, carrot, green beans, potatoes, tomatoes, beans, basil, and oregano. Bring just to a boil. Reduce heat to medium-low, cover, and simmer 20 minutes.

3 Add orzo and simmer another 8–10 minutes just until orzo is cooked. Season with salt and pepper.

4 Serve immediately.

Hot and Sour Soup

TRADITIONAL INGREDIENTS

If this Americanized version of hot and sour soup just doesn't satisfy your Szechuan cravings, hit up an Asian grocery store for some traditional ingredients. Replace the cabbage with ½ cup dried lily buds, substitute half of the shiitake mushrooms with wood ear fungus, and add a healthy shake of white pepper and chili oil.

If you can't get enough of traditional Chinese-American takeout, this is the soup for you.

2 tablespoons vegetable oil

2 cups diced seitan

1½ teaspoons hot sauce

6 cups vegetable broth

½ small head Napa cabbage, cored and shredded

¾ cup sliced shiitake mushrooms

1 (5-ounce) can bamboo shoots, drained

2 tablespoons soy sauce

2 tablespoons distilled white vinegar

¾ teaspoon crushed red pepper flakes

¾ teaspoon salt

2 tablespoons cornstarch

¼ cup water

3 scallions, trimmed and sliced

2 teaspoons sesame oil

1 In a large skillet, heat oil over medium heat. Add seitan and sauté 2–3 minutes until browned. Reduce heat to low and add hot sauce, stirring well to coat. Cook over low heat 1 more minute, then remove from heat and set aside.

2 In a stockpot or Dutch oven over medium-high heat, combine broth, cabbage, mushrooms, bamboo shoots, soy sauce, vinegar, red pepper flakes, and salt. Bring to a boil. Reduce heat to medium-low, cover, and simmer 15 minutes. Stir in seitan.

3 In a small bowl, whisk together cornstarch and water, then slowly stir into soup. Continue to cook, stirring, about 2 minutes until soup thickens.

4 Ladle into serving bowls, then top each serving with scallions and drizzle with sesame oil.

CHAPTER 6

Vegetables, Stir-Fries, and Sides

Orange-Ginger Stir-Fry

Rice vinegar can be substituted for the apple cider vinegar if you prefer. As with most stir-fry recipes, the vegetables are merely a suggestion; use your favorites or whatever you have in your refrigerator.

SERVES 4

Per Serving:

Calories	129
Fat	7g
Sodium	480mg
Carbohydrates	15g
Fiber	2g
Sugar	7g
Protein	4g

MAKE IT A NOODLE STIR-FRY

When stir-frying a saucy dish, you can add quick-cooking Asian-style noodles right into the pan. Add some extra sauce ingredients, ¼ to ⅓ cup water, and the noodles. Stir everything together and keep the heat low so the vegetables don't overcook. You've saved time—and an extra pan!

3 tablespoons orange juice

1 tablespoon apple cider vinegar

2 tablespoons soy sauce

2 tablespoons water

1 tablespoon maple syrup

1 teaspoon ground ginger

2 tablespoons vegetable oil

1 medium head broccoli, trimmed and chopped

½ cup sliced mushrooms

½ cup chopped snap peas

1 large carrot, peeled and sliced

1 cup chopped cabbage

2 cloves garlic, peeled and minced

1 In a small bowl, whisk together orange juice, vinegar, soy sauce, water, syrup, and ginger. Set aside.

2 In a large skillet, heat oil over medium heat. Add broccoli, mushrooms, peas, carrot, cabbage, and garlic. Sauté 2–3 minutes until vegetables are just starting to soften.

3 Add orange juice mixture and reduce heat to low. Simmer, stirring frequently, another 3–4 minutes until vegetables are tender. Serve immediately.

Creamed Spinach and Mushrooms

The combination of greens and nutritional yeast is simply delicious and provides an excellent jolt of nutrients that vegans need. Don't forget that spinach will shrink when cooked, so use lots!

2 tablespoons olive oil

1 small onion, peeled and diced

2 cloves garlic, peeled and minced

1½ cups sliced mushrooms

1 tablespoon all-purpose flour

2 bunches fresh spinach, trimmed

1 cup unsweetened soy milk

1 tablespoon vegan margarine

¼ teaspoon ground nutmeg

2 tablespoons nutritional yeast

½ teaspoon salt

¼ teaspoon ground black pepper

SERVES 4

Per Serving:

Calories	165
Fat	9g
Sodium	452mg
Carbohydrates	13g
Fiber	5g
Sugar	3g
Protein	8g

1 In a large skillet, heat oil over medium heat. Add onion, garlic, and mushrooms. Sauté 4 minutes. Add flour and heat, stirring constantly, 1 minute.

2 Reduce heat to medium-low and add spinach and soy milk. Cook uncovered 8–10 minutes until spinach is soft and liquid has reduced.

3 Stir in margarine, nutmeg, yeast, salt, and pepper. Serve immediately.

Chana Masala

SERVES 3

Per Serving:

Calories	231
Fat	5g
Sodium	930mg
Carbohydrates	38g
Fiber	10g
Sugar	12g
Protein	11g

This is a mild recipe suitable for the whole family, but if you want to turn up the heat, toss in some minced fresh chilies or a hearty dash of ground cayenne pepper. It's enjoyable as is for a side dish or piled on top of rice or another grain for a main meal.

2 tablespoons vegan margarine

1 medium onion, peeled and chopped

2 cloves garlic, peeled and minced

¾ teaspoon ground coriander

1 teaspoon ground cumin

1 (15-ounce) can chickpeas, undrained

⅔ cup tomato paste

½ teaspoon curry powder

¼ teaspoon ground turmeric

¼ teaspoon salt

1 tablespoon lemon juice

5 ounces baby spinach

1 In a large skillet, heat margarine over medium heat. Add onion and garlic and sauté 3–4 minutes until almost soft.

2 Reduce heat to medium-low and add coriander and cumin. Toast the spices, stirring, 1 minute.

3 Add chickpeas with liquid, tomato paste, curry powder, turmeric, and salt, and bring to a slow simmer. Cook 10–12 minutes until most of the liquid has been absorbed, stirring occasionally. Stir in lemon juice.

4 Add spinach and stir to combine. Cook about 1 minute, just until spinach wilts. Serve immediately.

Roasted Garlic Mashed Potatoes

Load up your mashed potatoes with a full head of roasted garlic for a flavor blast.

1 medium head garlic

2 tablespoons olive oil

1½ teaspoons salt, divided

6 medium Yukon Gold potatoes, peeled and cut into large chunks

¼ cup vegan margarine

½ cup soy heavy cream or unsweetened soy milk

¼ teaspoon ground white pepper

1 Preheat oven to 400°F.

2 Remove outer layer of skin from garlic head. Drizzle with olive oil, wrap in aluminum foil, and place on a baking sheet. Roast 30 minutes. Gently press cloves out of the skins into a small bowl and mash smooth with a fork.

3 Meanwhile, place potatoes in a large saucepan and cover with water. Add 1 teaspoon salt and bring to a boil over medium-high heat. Cook 15–20 minutes until tender.

4 Drain potatoes and transfer to a large bowl. Add roasted garlic, margarine, and cream and mash together using an electric mixer on low speed or a potato masher.

5 Season with pepper and remaining ½ teaspoon salt. Serve immediately.

SERVES 4

Per Serving:

Calories	403
Fat	18g
Sodium	976mg
Carbohydrates	53g
Fiber	5g
Sugar	2g
Protein	5g

VEGAN MASHED POTATO TRICKS

There's nothing wrong with just substituting vegan versions for the traditional butter and milk in your favorite potato recipe, but half a container of nondairy sour cream or cream cheese, a few teaspoons chopped fresh herbs, or some chopped artichoke hearts will make your potatoes come alive.

Roasted Brussels Sprouts with Apples

VARIATIONS

Change up this basic recipe by adding an extra ingredient or two each time you make it: chopped fresh rosemary, shredded vegan Parmesan cheese, chopped toasted nuts, or vegan bacon bits. For a Thanksgiving side dish, toss in some dried cranberries.

Brussels sprouts are surprisingly delicious when prepared properly. So if you have bad memories of being force-fed soggy, limp baby cabbages as a child, don't let that stop you from trying this recipe!

3 cups halved Brussels sprouts

8 cloves garlic, peeled

2 tablespoons olive oil

2 tablespoons balsamic vinegar

¾ teaspoon salt

½ teaspoon ground black pepper

2 large apples, cored and chopped

1 Preheat oven to 425°F.

2 Arrange Brussels sprouts and garlic in a single layer on a large baking sheet. Drizzle with olive oil and balsamic vinegar and season with salt and pepper. Roast 10 minutes, tossing once.

3 Remove tray from oven and add apples, tossing gently to combine. Roast 10 more minutes or until apples are soft, tossing once again. Serve warm.

Fiery Basil and Eggplant Stir-Fry

TYPES OF BASIL

Sweet Italian basil may be the most common, but other varieties can add a layer of sensually enticing flavor. Lemon basil has a lighter green color and fresh citrusy scent. Thai basil has purple leaves and stems, and the taste is sweet and similar to anise. There are two versions of holy basil—white and red—but both feature an intensely spicy flavor.

Holy basil, also called tulsi, *is revered in Vishnu temples across India and is frequently used in Ayurvedic healing. It lends a fantastically spicy flavor, but regular basil will also do.*

2 tablespoons olive oil

3 cloves garlic, peeled and minced

3 small fresh chili peppers, seeded and minced

1 (14-ounce) package firm or extra-firm tofu, drained, pressed, and diced

1 large eggplant, trimmed and chopped

1 medium red bell pepper, seeded and chopped

⅓ cup sliced mushrooms

3 tablespoons water

2 tablespoons soy sauce

1 teaspoon lemon juice

⅓ cup fresh holy basil leaves

1 In a large skillet, heat oil over medium-high heat. Add garlic, chilies, and tofu. Sauté 4–6 minutes until tofu is lightly golden.

2 Add eggplant, bell pepper, mushrooms, water, and soy sauce. Cook, stirring frequently, 5–6 minutes until eggplant is almost soft.

3 Add lemon juice and basil and sauté 1–2 minutes until basil is wilted. Serve hot.

Potatoes "Au Gratin"

You'll never miss the boxed version after trying these easy potatoes! Replace the bread crumbs with crushed French-fried onions for a fun twist on an old favorite.

4 large russet potatoes, sliced into thin coins

1 medium onion, peeled and chopped

1 tablespoon vegan margarine

2 tablespoons all-purpose flour

2 cups unsweetened soy milk

2 teaspoons onion powder

1 teaspoon garlic powder

2 tablespoons nutritional yeast

1 teaspoon lemon juice

½ teaspoon salt

¾ teaspoon paprika

½ teaspoon ground black pepper

¾ cup plain bread crumbs

SERVES 4	
Per Serving:	
Calories	472
Fat	3g
Sodium	565mg
Carbohydrates	91g
Fiber	10g
Sugar	9g
Protein	16g

1 Preheat oven to 375°F.

2 Arrange half of potato slices in a 2-quart casserole or baking dish. Layer half of chopped onion on top of potatoes.

3 In a small saucepan, melt margarine over low heat. Add flour, stirring to make a paste. Stir in soy milk, onion powder, garlic powder, yeast, lemon juice, and salt. Cook 2–3 minutes, stirring constantly, until sauce has thickened.

4 Pour half of sauce over potatoes and onion, then layer the remaining potatoes and onion on top of sauce. Pour remaining sauce on top. Sprinkle with paprika and pepper and top with bread crumbs.

5 Cover and bake 45 minutes. Remove cover and bake an additional 10 minutes. Serve hot.

Green Bean Amandine

SERVES 4

Per Serving:

Calories	155
Fat	11g
Sodium	7mg
Carbohydrates	12g
Fiber	5g
Sugar	5g
Protein	5g

Fresh green beans are so much tastier than the frozen or canned variety. Almonds and mushrooms are classic green bean companions.

1 pound green beans, trimmed and chopped

2 tablespoons olive oil

⅓ cup sliced almonds

¾ cup sliced mushrooms

1 small onion, peeled and chopped

1 teaspoon lemon juice

1 In a medium saucepan fitted with a steamer insert, heat 1" water over medium-high heat to boiling. Place green beans in the steamer, cover, and steam 5 minutes. Drain beans and rinse under cold water.

2 In a large skillet, heat oil over medium heat. Add almonds, mushrooms, and onion. Sauté 3 minutes. Add green beans and lemon juice and heat 2 minutes.

3 Serve immediately.

Lemon-Mint New Potatoes

Potatoes make an easy side dish that goes with just about any entrée, and this version with fresh mint adds a twist to the usual herb-roasted version.

12 small new potatoes, quartered

4 cloves garlic, peeled and minced

1 tablespoon olive oil

¼ cup chopped fresh mint

½ teaspoon salt

½ teaspoon ground black pepper

2 teaspoons lemon juice

1 Preheat oven to 350°F. Line a baking sheet with parchment paper or spray it with nonstick cooking spray.

2 In a large bowl, toss together potatoes, garlic, oil, and mint, stirring to coat.

3 Arrange potato mixture in a single layer on prepared baking sheet. Roast 45 minutes.

4 Season with salt and pepper and drizzle with lemon juice just before serving.

SERVES 4

Per Serving:

Calories	175
Fat	3g
Sodium	306mg
Carbohydrates	33g
Fiber	4g
Sugar	2g
Protein	4g

MEAL PREP TIP

While you're roasting potatoes for dinner, make a double batch to use for a Greek-inspired potato salad for lunch the next day. Cool the potatoes, then combine with ¼ cup vegan yogurt, green peas, diced red onions or celery, and some chopped fresh mint.

Pan-Fried Tofu

Serve this simple fried tofu with just about any dipping sauce for a snack, or add it to salads or stir-fries instead of plain tofu.

¼ cup soy sauce

1 (14-ounce) package firm or extra-firm tofu, drained, pressed, and cubed

2 tablespoons all-purpose flour

2 tablespoons nutritional yeast

1 teaspoon garlic powder

¼ teaspoon salt

¼ teaspoon ground black pepper

3 tablespoons vegetable oil

1 In a medium bowl, combine soy sauce with tofu and set aside to marinate at least 1 hour.

2 In a shallow bowl, combine flour, yeast, garlic powder, salt, and pepper.

3 In a large skillet, heat oil over medium-high heat.

4 Using tongs, transfer tofu cubes to flour mixture and toss until coated. Transfer to skillet and fry 4–5 minutes in a single layer until crispy and lightly golden brown on all sides.

5 Drain on paper towels and serve warm or at room temperature.

Air-Fried Tofu

Serve these crispy, protein-rich cubes with rice or steamed vegetables and a simple sauce. You can also add them to salads, or even enjoy them plain with a favorite dipping sauce.

1 (14-ounce) package extra-firm tofu, drained, pressed, and cubed
2 teaspoons olive oil
¼ teaspoon salt

1 Preheat air fryer to 375°F and set timer for 18 minutes.
2 Remove fryer basket and spray with nonstick cooking spray. Add tofu cubes and olive oil. Toss to coat, then place basket back in air fryer.
3 Every 5 minutes, remove basket and stir tofu by shaking basket carefully. Cook until timer goes off and tofu is crispy. Remove from basket and sprinkle with salt.
4 Serve hot or at room temperature.

SERVES 4

Per Serving:

Calories	89
Fat	6g
Sodium	157mg
Carbohydrates	2g
Fiber	1g
Sugar	1g
Protein	8g

Coconut-Cauliflower Curry

To save time chopping, substitute a bag of frozen mixed vegetables or toss in some leftover cooked potatoes. Serve this tropical yellow curry over brown rice or another whole grain.

¾ cup vegetable broth

1 cup canned coconut milk

1½ cups frozen green peas

1 large head cauliflower, cored and chopped

2 medium carrots, peeled and diced

2 teaspoons minced fresh ginger

3 cloves garlic, peeled and minced

2 teaspoons curry powder

½ teaspoon ground turmeric

1 teaspoon light brown sugar

¼ teaspoon salt

¼ teaspoon ground nutmeg

1 cup diced fresh or drained canned pineapple

2 tablespoons chopped fresh cilantro

SERVES 4

Per Serving:

Calories	246
Fat	12g
Sodium	441mg
Carbohydrates	30g
Fiber	9g
Sugar	14g
Protein	9g

1 In a large saucepan over medium-high heat, whisk together broth and coconut milk.
2 Add peas, cauliflower, carrots, ginger, garlic, curry powder, turmeric, brown sugar, salt, and nutmeg, stirring well to combine. Bring to a boil.
3 Reduce heat to low, cover, and simmer 8–10 minutes, stirring occasionally. Stir in pineapple and heat 2 more minutes.
4 Top with cilantro and serve hot.

Pineapple-Cabbage Stir-Fry

SERVES 6

Per Serving:

Calories	250
Fat	12g
Sodium	346mg
Carbohydrates	29g
Fiber	4g
Sugar	16g
Protein	10g

The sweet, spicy, and salty sauce in this stir-fry is irresistible. Serve it over Coconut Rice (see recipe in Chapter 7) for a tropical treat.

1 (15-ounce) can diced pineapple packed in juice, drained (juice reserved)

2 tablespoons red wine vinegar

1 tablespoon soy sauce

1 tablespoon light brown sugar

2 teaspoons cornstarch

¼ teaspoon crushed red pepper flakes

2 tablespoons olive oil

1 small onion, peeled and chopped

2 cloves garlic, peeled and minced

1 large head broccoli, trimmed and cut into florets

1 small head Napa cabbage, cored and chopped

1 batch Pan-Fried Tofu (see recipe in this chapter)

1 In a small bowl, whisk together reserved pineapple juice, vinegar, soy sauce, brown sugar, cornstarch, and red pepper flakes.

2 In a large wok or skillet, heat oil over medium-high heat. Add onion and garlic and sauté 3–4 minutes just until soft. Add broccoli, pineapple, and cabbage and stir-fry another minute.

3 Reduce heat to medium and stir in pineapple juice mixture. Cook, stirring, just until mixture has thickened, about 1 minute.

4 Add tofu and stir about 1 minute more until heated through. Serve hot.

Cranberry-Apple Stuffing

Why wait for Thanksgiving? Stuffing is a fabulous side dish anytime. The herbs will scent your kitchen with a lovely aroma.

3 tablespoons vegan margarine

1 medium onion, peeled and diced

2 stalks celery, diced

2/3 cup sliced mushrooms

3/4 teaspoon ground sage

3/4 teaspoon dried thyme

1/2 teaspoon ground marjoram

12 slices stale bread, cubed

1 cup dried cranberries

1 large apple, peeled, cored, and diced

1/2 cup apple juice

2 cups vegetable broth

1/2 teaspoon salt

1/4 teaspoon ground black pepper

1 Preheat oven to 375°F.

2 In a large skillet, melt margarine over medium heat. Add onion, celery, and mushrooms. Sauté 4–5 minutes until mushrooms and onion are soft. Add sage, thyme, and marjoram. Cook 1 minute. Transfer to a large bowl.

3 Add bread, cranberries, apple, and apple juice. Gradually add broth until the mixture is moistened but not too wet. You may need a little more or less than 2 cups. Season with salt and pepper.

4 Transfer to a large casserole or baking dish and bake 25 minutes. Serve hot.

SERVES 6

Per Serving:

Calories	282
Fat	4g
Sodium	807mg
Carbohydrates	55g
Fiber	4g
Sugar	23g
Protein	6g

PLUMP BERRIES

For an extra-moist and sweet stuffing, rehydrate the dried cranberries first. Place them in a small bowl and cover them with apple, orange, or pineapple juice and set them aside about 15 minutes until soft and plumped up. If you want to get fancy, use a fruit liqueur instead of juice.

Garlic and Ginger Green Beans

SERVES 4

Per Serving:

Calories	98
Fat	7g
Sodium	152mg
Carbohydrates	9g
Fiber	3g
Sugar	4g
Protein	2g

Fresh green beans, lightly steamed so they're still crisp, are cooked simply with garlic, ginger, and crushed red pepper flakes.

1 pound green beans, trimmed and chopped

2 tablespoons olive oil

4 cloves garlic, peeled and minced

1 teaspoon minced fresh ginger

½ teaspoon crushed red pepper flakes

¼ teaspoon salt

⅛ teaspoon ground black pepper

1 In a medium saucepan fitted with a steamer insert, heat 1" water over medium-high heat to boiling. Place green beans in the steamer, cover, and steam 5 minutes. Drain and rinse under cold water.

2 In a medium skillet, heat oil over medium heat. Add garlic, ginger, green beans, and red pepper flakes. Sauté 3–4 minutes, stirring frequently, until garlic is soft.

3 Season with salt and pepper and serve.

Kung Pao Cauliflower

This stir-fried cauliflower recipe is seasoned with a sweet and spicy kung pao sauce. It is a classic Chinese takeout dish, transformed into healthier (yet still delicious) fare thanks to the cauliflower.

½ cup all-purpose flour

1 teaspoon baking soda

¾ cup unsweetened almond milk

1 medium head cauliflower, cored and cut into florets

½ cup crushed cornflakes

3 tablespoons tamari soy sauce

3 tablespoons agave nectar

1 tablespoon sesame oil

1 teaspoon rice vinegar

1 teaspoon garlic powder

1 teaspoon ground ginger

1 tablespoon cornstarch

1 tablespoon finely chopped fresh cilantro

2 tablespoons sesame seeds

SERVES 4

Per Serving:

Calories	229
Fat	6g
Sodium	1,198mg
Carbohydrates	38g
Fiber	5g
Sugar	11g
Protein	8g

1 Preheat oven to 400°F. Line a large baking sheet with parchment paper.

2 In a large bowl, combine flour, baking soda, and almond milk. Add cauliflower florets and stir until florets are coated. Sprinkle with crushed cornflakes and toss again to coat. Place coated cauliflower florets on prepared baking sheet, allowing space between each piece.

3 Bake 15 minutes. Remove from oven and transfer to a large bowl. Set aside.

4 In a small microwave-safe bowl, combine tamari, agave, oil, vinegar, garlic powder, ginger, and cornstarch. Microwave on high 30 seconds. Remove and stir. Repeat until sauce begins to bubble and thicken.

5 Pour sauce over cauliflower and stir gently to coat. Pour cauliflower back onto baking sheet and bake 15 minutes.

6 Set aside to cool 2 minutes. Top with cilantro and sesame seeds and serve immediately.

Mango and Bell Pepper Stir-Fry

SERVES 4

Per Serving:

Calories	169
Fat	7g
Sodium	794mg
Carbohydrates	24g
Fiber	4g
Sugar	16g
Protein	4g

Enjoy this fresh and sweet stir-fry for a light lunch, or add some marinated tofu and brown rice to make it a satisfying dinner.

2 tablespoons lime juice

2 tablespoons orange juice

1 tablespoon hot sauce

3 tablespoons soy sauce

2 tablespoons vegetable oil

2 cloves garlic, peeled and minced

1 large red bell pepper, seeded and sliced

1 large orange bell pepper, seeded and sliced

1 medium head broccoli, trimmed and chopped

1 large mango, peeled, pitted, and cubed

3 medium scallions, trimmed and chopped

1 In a small bowl, whisk together lime juice, orange juice, hot sauce, and soy sauce.

2 In a large skillet, heat oil over medium-high heat. Add garlic and sauté 1 minute, then add bell peppers and broccoli. Cook, stirring frequently, another 2–3 minutes until slightly softened.

3 Stir in soy sauce mixture, reduce heat to medium-low, and cook another 2–3 minutes until broccoli and bell peppers are tender.

4 Reduce heat to low and add mango and scallions, gently stirring to combine. Heat 1–2 minutes until mango is warmed. Serve immediately.

Maple-Glazed Roasted Vegetables

SERVES 4

Per Serving:

Calories	299
Fat	8g
Sodium	576mg
Carbohydrates	55g
Fiber	8g
Sugar	28g
Protein	4g

ROOT LOVE

This tangy, sweet glaze is delicious and works well with a variety of roasted vegetables. Try it with Brussels sprouts, beets, baby new potatoes, butternut or acorn squash, turnips, or daikon radish.

This makes an excellent holiday side dish. The vegetables can be roasted in advance and reheated with the glaze to save on time if needed.

3 large carrots, peeled and chopped

2 small parsnips, peeled and chopped

2 medium sweet potatoes, peeled and chopped

2 tablespoons olive oil

½ teaspoon salt

½ teaspoon ground black pepper

⅓ cup maple syrup

2 tablespoons Dijon mustard

1 tablespoon balsamic vinegar

½ teaspoon hot sauce

1 Preheat oven to 400°F.
2 Spread out carrots, parsnips, and sweet potatoes on a large baking sheet. Drizzle with oil and sprinkle with salt and pepper. Roast 40 minutes, tossing once.
3 In a large bowl, whisk together syrup, mustard, vinegar, and hot sauce.
4 Transfer roasted vegetables to bowl and toss to coat with syrup mixture. Serve immediately.

CHAPTER 7

Rice and Grains

Italian White Beans and Rice

This is a quick, inexpensive, and hearty meal that will quickly become a favorite standby on busy nights. It's nutritious and filling, and can easily be doubled for a crowd.

SERVES 4

Per Serving:

Calories	316
Fat	8g
Sodium	474mg
Carbohydrates	52g
Fiber	8g
Sugar	6g
Protein	9g

2 tablespoons olive oil

1 small onion, peeled and diced

2 stalks celery, diced

3 cloves garlic, peeled and minced

1 (14.5-ounce) can diced tomatoes

1 (15-ounce) can cannellini beans, drained and rinsed

½ teaspoon dried parsley

½ teaspoon dried basil

2 cups cooked white rice

1 tablespoon balsamic vinegar

1 In a large skillet, heat oil over medium-high heat. Add onion, celery, and garlic. Sauté 4–5 minutes until onion and celery are soft.

2 Reduce heat to medium-low and add tomatoes, beans, parsley, and basil. Cover and simmer 10 minutes, stirring occasionally.

3 Stir in rice and vinegar and cook uncovered 2–3 minutes until liquid is absorbed. Serve immediately.

Spicy Jambalaya

Make this spicy and smoky southern rice dish a main meal by adding in some browned vegan sausage or sautéed tofu.

2 tablespoons olive oil

1 small onion, peeled and chopped

1 medium red bell pepper, seeded and chopped

1 stalk celery, diced

1 (14.5-ounce) can diced tomatoes

3 cups vegetable broth

2 cups uncooked white rice

1 bay leaf

1 teaspoon paprika

½ teaspoon dried thyme

½ teaspoon dried oregano

½ teaspoon garlic powder

1 cup corn kernels

½ teaspoon ground cayenne pepper

1 In a large saucepan or Dutch oven, heat oil over medium-high heat. Add onion, bell pepper, and celery. Sauté 3–4 minutes until almost soft.

2 Reduce heat to medium-low and add tomatoes, broth, rice, bay leaf, paprika, thyme, oregano, and garlic powder. Cover and simmer 20 minutes until rice is tender, stirring occasionally.

3 Stir in corn and cayenne pepper and cook about 3 minutes just until heated through. Remove bay leaf before serving.

SERVES 6

Per Serving:

Calories	330
Fat	5g
Sodium	535mg
Carbohydrates	64g
Fiber	3g
Sugar	6g
Protein	6g

LEFTOVER HACK

Leftover Jambalaya can be used to make fusion burritos. Spoon the mixture onto tortillas and top with vegan refried beans, salsa, and shredded lettuce.

Sun-Dried Tomato Risotto

The tomatoes carry the flavor in this easy risotto. But if you have some fancy oil on hand—truffle, hazelnut, pine nut, or walnut—now's the time to use it. Just replace the margarine with the flavored oil.

5½ cups vegetable broth, divided

2 tablespoons olive oil

1 medium onion, peeled and diced

4 cloves garlic, peeled and minced

1½ cups uncooked Arborio rice

⅔ cup rehydrated sun-dried tomatoes, sliced

2 cups baby spinach

1 tablespoon chopped fresh basil

2 tablespoons vegan margarine

2 tablespoons nutritional yeast

½ teaspoon salt

½ teaspoon ground black pepper

¼ cup pine nuts

SERVES 4

Per Serving:

Calories	460
Fat	14g
Sodium	1,168mg
Carbohydrates	71g
Fiber	4g
Sugar	6g
Protein	9g

INCREASE THE SUN-DRIED TOMATO FLAVOR

If you're using dehydrated tomatoes, rehydrate them first by covering them in water at least 10 minutes, and add the soaking water to the broth. You can also make this risotto with tomatoes packed in oil. If you do, add 2 tablespoons of the oil to the risotto at the end of cooking instead of the vegan margarine.

1 In a medium saucepan over medium heat, place 5 cups broth. Bring to a simmer, then reduce heat to low.

2 In a large saucepan or Dutch oven, heat oil over medium heat. Add onion and garlic and sauté 3–4 minutes just until soft. Add rice and toast 1 minute, stirring constantly.

3 Add ¾ cup of the hot broth and stir to combine. When most of the liquid has been absorbed, add another ½ cup, stirring constantly. Continue adding broth ¼–½ cup at a time, stirring until most of liquid is absorbed after each addition, about 20 minutes, until rice is just tender and sauce is creamy.

4 Add tomatoes, spinach, basil, and remaining ½ cup broth and reduce heat to low. Stir to combine. Cook, stirring, 3–4 minutes until tomatoes are soft and spinach is wilted.

5 Stir in margarine, yeast, salt, and pepper.

6 Remove from heat and set aside to cool 5 minutes. Top with pine nuts. Serve immediately.

Cuban Black Bean and Sweet Potato Bowls

SERVES 4

Per Serving:

Calories	467
Fat	8g
Sodium	831mg
Carbohydrates	83g
Fiber	19g
Sugar	7g
Protein	17g

These nourishing bowls are wonderful on their own, but you can add whatever you like to them. Roasted vegetables, chopped nuts, or sliced avocados are some good ideas.

2 tablespoons olive oil

3 cloves garlic, peeled and minced

2 large sweet potatoes, peeled and diced

2 (15-ounce) cans black beans, drained and rinsed

¾ cup vegetable broth

1 tablespoon chili powder

1 teaspoon paprika

1 teaspoon ground cumin

1 tablespoon lime juice

1 tablespoon hot sauce

2 cups cooked white rice

1 In a large saucepan or Dutch oven, heat oil over medium-high heat. Add garlic and sweet potatoes and sauté 3 minutes.

2 Reduce heat to medium-low and add beans, broth, chili powder, paprika, and cumin. Cover and simmer 25–30 minutes until sweet potatoes are soft.

3 Stir in lime juice and hot sauce. Serve hot over rice.

Fried Rice with Tofu and Cashews

On busy weeknights, pick up some plain white rice from a Chinese takeout restaurant and use it to make a healthy homemade fried rice dish. Garnish the rice with fresh lime wedges.

3 tablespoons olive oil, divided

2 cloves garlic, peeled and minced

1 (14-ounce) package silken tofu, drained and mashed with a fork

3 cups cooked white rice

½ cup frozen peas

3 tablespoons soy sauce

1 tablespoon sesame oil

2 tablespoons lime juice

3 scallions, trimmed and sliced

⅓ cup chopped cashews

1 In a large skillet or wok, heat 2 tablespoons olive oil over medium-high heat. Add garlic and tofu and sauté 6–8 minutes until tofu is lightly browned.

2 Stir in remaining 1 tablespoon olive oil, rice, peas, soy sauce, and sesame oil. Cook 4 minutes, stirring constantly.

3 Remove from heat and stir in lime juice, scallions, and cashews. Serve immediately.

SERVES 3

Per Serving:

Calories	605
Fat	28g
Sodium	955mg
Carbohydrates	68g
Fiber	3g
Sugar	4g
Protein	19g

QUICK HEALTHY MEALS

Like stir-fries and an easy pasta recipe, fried rice is a quick and easy meal you can turn to again and again. The formula is always the same: rice, oil, and seasonings, but the variations are endless. Besides tofu, try adding tempeh, seitan, or other meat substitutes. Add kimchi for Korean spice, or season the rice with a mixture of cumin, curry, ginger, and turmeric for an Indian-inspired dish.

Coconut Rice

Serve Coconut Rice as a simple side dish or pair it with spicy Thai and Indian curries or stir-fries.

SERVES 4

Per Serving:

Calories	492
Fat	24g
Sodium	306mg
Carbohydrates	60g
Fiber	2g
Sugar	1g
Protein	7g

TOASTED COCONUT FLAKES

Quickly toasting coconut flakes will help bring out their nutty flavor. Place the flakes in a dry skillet over low heat. Stirring constantly, heat the coconut just until you see the slightest bit of golden brown, then remove the pan from the heat.

1 cup water

1 (14-ounce) can coconut milk

1½ cups uncooked white rice

⅓ cup unsweetened coconut flakes

1 teaspoon lime juice

½ teaspoon salt

1 In a large saucepan over medium-high heat, combine water, coconut milk, and rice and bring to a boil. Reduce heat to low, cover, and simmer 20 minutes, or until rice is tender.

2 In a small skillet over low heat, toast coconut flakes about 3 minutes until lightly golden. Gently stir constantly to avoid burning.

3 Add coconut flakes to cooked rice and stir in lime juice and salt. Serve immediately.

Lemon Rice with Spinach

Greek spanakorizo is seasoned with fresh lemon, herbs, and black pepper. Serve it with Lemon-Basil Tofu (see recipe in Chapter 10) for a citrusy meal.

2 tablespoons olive oil

1 small onion, peeled and chopped

4 cloves garlic, peeled and minced

¾ cup uncooked white rice

2½ cups water

1 (8-ounce) can tomato paste

5 ounces baby spinach

2 tablespoons chopped fresh parsley

1 tablespoon chopped fresh mint

2 tablespoons lemon juice

½ teaspoon salt

½ teaspoon ground black pepper

1 In a large saucepan, heat oil over medium-high heat. Add onion and garlic and sauté 3 minutes, then add rice, stirring to lightly toast. Add water and bring to a boil. Reduce heat to medium-low, cover, and simmer 10 minutes.

2 Add tomato paste, spinach, and parsley. Cover and simmer another 5 minutes until spinach is wilted and rice is tender.

3 Stir in mint, lemon juice, salt, and pepper. Serve warm.

SERVES 4

Per Serving:

Calories	254
Fat	7g
Sodium	769mg
Carbohydrates	43g
Fiber	4g
Sugar	8g
Protein	6g

Acorn Squash and Sage Risotto

SERVES 4

Per Serving:

Calories	396
Fat	7g
Sodium	1,152mg
Carbohydrates	76g
Fiber	5g
Sugar	3g
Protein	6g

QUICKER AND CREAMIER

When making risotto, keep the broth simmering on the stove next to the risotto as it cooks. Adding hot liquid will help the rice cook faster and ensures an evenly cooked rice with a creamy sauce.

This earthy recipe works well with just about any kind of squash. If you're in a hurry, use canned puréed pumpkin instead of fresh acorn squash or look for precooked butternut squash in your grocer's freezer section.

5¼ cups vegetable broth, divided

2 tablespoons olive oil

1 small onion, peeled and diced

3 cloves garlic, peeled and minced

1½ cups uncooked Arborio rice

2 whole cloves

1½ cups roasted puréed acorn squash

1½ teaspoons ground sage

¼ teaspoon salt

¼ teaspoon ground black pepper

1 In a medium saucepan over medium heat, place 5 cups broth. Bring to a simmer, then reduce heat to low.

2 In a large saucepan, heat oil over medium-high heat. Add onion and garlic and sauté 3–4 minutes just until soft. Add rice and toast 1 minute, stirring constantly.

3 Add cloves and ¾ cup hot broth and stir to combine. When most of the liquid has been absorbed, add another ½ cup broth, stirring constantly. Continue adding broth ¼–½ cup at a time, stirring until most of liquid is absorbed after each addition, about 20–25 minutes, until rice is just tender and sauce is creamy.

4 Reduce heat to medium-low and stir in squash and remaining ¼ cup vegetable broth. Continue to stir and cook 5 more minutes.

5 Stir in sage, salt, and pepper and remove from heat.

6 Set aside to cool, stirring occasionally, at least 5 minutes. Risotto will thicken slightly as it cools. Remove cloves before serving.

Nasi Goreng (Indonesian Fried Rice)

As in any fried rice recipe, the vegetables you use here are really up to you.

2 teaspoons molasses

2 tablespoons soy sauce

3 tablespoons peanut oil

1 (8-ounce) package tempeh, cubed

1 small onion, peeled and diced

3 cloves garlic, peeled and minced

1 small red chili pepper, seeded and minced

3 cups cooked white rice

1 tablespoon sesame oil

2 tablespoons ketchup

2 tablespoons hot sauce

2 scallions, trimmed and chopped

1 large carrot, peeled and thinly sliced

1 medium red or yellow bell pepper, seeded and diced

¼ teaspoon Chinese five-spice powder

1 In a small bowl, whisk together molasses and soy sauce; set aside.

2 In a large skillet, heat peanut oil over medium-high heat. Add tempeh, onion, garlic, and chili. Sauté 2–3 minutes until tempeh is lightly browned. Stir in rice and sesame oil.

3 Add ketchup, hot sauce, scallions, carrot, bell pepper, five-spice powder, and molasses mixture. Stir quickly to combine.

4 Cook 2–3 minutes, stirring constantly, just until heated through. Serve immediately.

SERVES 6

Per Serving:

Calories	292
Fat	12g
Sodium	513mg
Carbohydrates	34g
Fiber	2g
Sugar	5g
Protein	10g

A WARUNG FAVORITE

In *warungs* (restaurants) across Indonesia, nasi goreng is guaranteed to be on the menu, and it's a favorite of visitors and locals alike. Top it off with some extra hot sauce to spice it up or serve it with sliced cucumbers to temper the hot chili. Asian grocery stores sell kecap manis, a sugary sauce you can use in place of the soy sauce and molasses mixture for a more authentic Indonesian taste.

Red Beans and Rice

Cook the beans from scratch and use the cooking liquid instead of vegetable broth if you've got the time.

3 cloves garlic, peeled

1 small onion, peeled and chopped

3 stalks celery, chopped

2 tablespoons chopped fresh parsley

2 tablespoons olive oil

½ teaspoon dried rosemary

½ teaspoon dried thyme

¼ teaspoon ground cloves

1 (15-ounce) can kidney beans, drained and rinsed

3 cups vegetable broth

2 bay leaves

1½ cups uncooked white rice

¼ teaspoon salt

½ teaspoon ground black pepper

1 Place garlic, onion, celery, and parsley in a food processor and pulse until finely minced.

2 In a large saucepan, heat oil over medium-high heat. Add onion mixture and sauté 3–4 minutes until soft. Add rosemary, thyme, cloves, and beans, stirring to combine. Cook 2 more minutes until fragrant.

3 Reduce heat to medium-low and add broth, bay leaves, and rice. Bring to a slow simmer, cover, and cook 30 minutes.

4 Reduce heat to low, uncover, and cook 10 more minutes, or until most of the liquid is absorbed. Season with salt and pepper.

5 Remove bay leaves before serving.

Cranberry-Apple Wild Rice

SERVES 4

Per Serving:

Calories	427
Fat	17g
Sodium	905mg
Carbohydrates	61g
Fiber	6g
Sugar	22g
Protein	9g

A HIGH-PROTEIN OPTION

Wild rice is not actually rice—it's a seed. With almost 7 grams of protein per cup when cooked, wild rice can be an excellent source of protein. Add ¼ cup wild rice per cup of white rice to any recipe that calls for regular white rice for an extra protein boost.

To speed up the cooking time, soak the wild rice 15–20 minutes before boiling.

2 tablespoons olive oil

1 stalk celery, diced

1 large red onion, peeled and diced

1 cup uncooked wild rice

3 cups vegetable broth

⅓ cup orange juice

½ cup dried cranberries

½ cup pine nuts

2 scallions, trimmed and chopped

1 large apple, cored and diced

½ teaspoon salt

¼ teaspoon ground black pepper

1 In a large saucepan or Dutch oven, heat oil over medium-high heat. Add celery and onion and sauté 4–5 minutes until soft.

2 Add wild rice and broth and bring to a boil. Reduce heat to low, cover, and simmer 30 minutes. Add orange juice and simmer another 10–15 minutes until rice is tender.

3 Remove from heat and stir in cranberries. Cover and set aside 5 minutes.

4 Add pine nuts, scallions, apple, salt, and pepper. Toss to combine. Serve hot or cold.

Barley and Mushroom Pilaf

This earthy-flavored pilaf with mushrooms and nutty toasted barley is a filling dish that's perfect for that first chilly fall evening.

3 tablespoons vegan margarine, divided

1 cup sliced porcini mushrooms

1 cup sliced shiitake mushrooms

2 stalks celery, diced

1 small onion, peeled and chopped

1¼ cups uncooked barley

3¾ cups vegetable broth

1 bay leaf

¼ teaspoon ground sage

½ teaspoon dried parsley

½ teaspoon dried thyme

1 In a large saucepan or Dutch oven, melt 2 tablespoons margarine over medium-high heat. Add mushrooms, celery, and onion. Sauté 3–4 minutes until almost soft. Add barley and remaining 1 tablespoon margarine and cook 1–2 minutes, stirring frequently, until barley starts to brown.

2 Add broth, bay leaf, sage, parsley, and thyme. Bring to a boil. Reduce heat to low, cover, and simmer 20–25 minutes, stirring occasionally, until liquid is absorbed and barley is tender. Remove bay leaf before serving.

SERVES 4

Per Serving:

Calories	287
Fat	4g
Sodium	838mg
Carbohydrates	56g
Fiber	11g
Sugar	4g
Protein	8g

COOKING BARLEY

Be sure you pick up either pearl or quick-cooking barley, and not the hulled variety, which takes a long time to cook. Pearl barley is done in 20–25 minutes, and quick-cooking barley is done in about 10 minutes, so adjust the cooking times as needed. Barley can also be cooked in a rice steamer with about 2½ cups liquid for each 1 cup barley.

Mediterranean Quinoa Pilaf

SERVES 4

Per Serving:

Calories	375
Fat	14g
Sodium	1,180mg
Carbohydrates	50g
Fiber	6g
Sugar	6g
Protein	10g

Bring this vibrant, Mediterranean-inspired whole-grain entrée to a potluck and watch it magically disappear.

1½ cups uncooked white or red quinoa

3 cups vegetable broth

3 tablespoons balsamic vinegar

2 tablespoons olive oil

1 tablespoon lemon juice

¼ teaspoon salt

½ cup chopped sun-dried tomatoes

½ cup chopped artichoke hearts

½ cup chopped Kalamata olives

1 In a large saucepan or Dutch oven over high heat, combine quinoa and broth. Bring to a boil. Reduce heat to low, cover, and simmer about 15 minutes until liquid is absorbed. Remove from heat, fluff quinoa with a fork, and set aside 5 minutes.

2 Stir in vinegar, oil, lemon juice, salt, tomatoes, artichokes, and olives, gently tossing to combine. Serve hot.

Quinoa and Herb Stuffing

Substitute dried herbs if you have to, but fresh is best in this untraditional stuffing recipe.

¼ cup vegan margarine

1 medium onion, peeled and chopped

2 stalks celery, diced

1 teaspoon chopped fresh rosemary

2 teaspoons chopped fresh marjoram

1½ tablespoons chopped fresh thyme

1 tablespoon chopped fresh sage

6 slices stale bread, cubed

1¼ cups vegetable broth

2 cups cooked white or red quinoa

¾ teaspoon salt

½ teaspoon ground black pepper

1 Preheat oven to 400°F. Spray a 9" × 13" baking dish with nonstick cooking spray.

2 In a medium skillet, melt margarine over medium-high heat. Add onion and celery and sauté 4–5 minutes until soft. Add rosemary, marjoram, thyme, and sage. Heat 1 minute until fragrant.

3 Remove from heat and stir in bread. Add broth to moisten bread; you may need a bit more or less than 1¼ cups.

4 Add cooked quinoa, salt, and pepper, and stir to combine. Transfer to prepared baking dish.

5 Cover and bake 30 minutes. Serve warm.

SERVES 6

Per Serving:

Calories	197
Fat	5g
Sodium	673mg
Carbohydrates	31g
Fiber	3g
Sugar	4g
Protein	6g

STUFFING TIPS

Stuffing works best with stale bread to better absorb all that flavor and moisture. Leave bread out for a couple of days, or lightly toast slices in a 275°F oven for 20 minutes on each side. For more variety, stir in ¾ cup chopped dried apricots and ¾ cup chopped nuts (walnuts, cashews, or pecans) before baking. Or sauté some sliced mushrooms or diced carrot along the with the onion and celery.

Baked Quinoa "Mac 'n' Cheese"

SUPER QUINOA

Quinoa is actually a seed, but it's considered a whole grain. A source of protein, fiber, and iron, it's also a superfood. Quinoa is gluten-free, a complete protein, and a source of flavonoid antioxidants. With its crunchy texture and nutty flavor, it's a healthy substitute for rice and other grains.

Craving the flavors of your childhood favorite, macaroni and cheese? Try this filling whole-grain substitute.

1½ cups uncooked white or red quinoa

3 cups vegetable broth

2 tablespoons olive oil

1 medium onion, peeled and chopped

3 cloves garlic, peeled and minced

2 cups chopped broccoli

1 large tomato, cored and diced

1 tablespoon all-purpose flour

¾ cup unsweetened soy milk

½ teaspoon salt

1 cup shredded vegan Cheddar cheese, divided

½ teaspoon dried parsley

1 cup seasoned bread crumbs

¼ teaspoon ground nutmeg

1 Preheat oven to 350°F. Spray a large casserole dish with nonstick cooking spray.

2 In a large saucepan or Dutch oven over high heat, combine quinoa and broth. Bring to a boil. Reduce heat to low, cover, and simmer about 15 minutes until liquid is absorbed. Remove from heat, fluff quinoa with a fork, and set aside 5 minutes.

3 In a medium skillet, heat oil over medium-high heat. Add onion and garlic and sauté 4–5 minutes until soft. Add broccoli and tomato and sauté 3 minutes.

4 Stir in flour, then add soy milk and salt. Cook about 3 minutes, stirring until thick. Transfer to a large bowl and add cooked quinoa and ½ cup vegan Cheddar. Mix until combined, then pour into prepared casserole dish.

5 Sprinkle with remaining ½ cup vegan Cheddar. Top with parsley, bread crumbs, and nutmeg. Bake 10–12 minutes until cheese is melted. Cool 5 minutes before serving.

Baked Millet Patties

Serve these nutty whole-grain patties topped with Mushroom Gravy (see recipe in Chapter 2).

1½ cups cooked millet

½ cup tahini

1 cup plain bread crumbs

1 teaspoon dried parsley

¾ teaspoon garlic powder

½ teaspoon onion powder

¼ teaspoon salt

1 Preheat oven to 350°F.
2 Combine all ingredients in a large bowl and stir to mix together well.
3 Use your hands to press firmly into eight (1") patties and place on a large baking sheet.
4 Bake 10 minutes on each side. Serve warm.

SERVES 8

Per Serving:

Calories	179
Fat	8g
Sodium	183mg
Carbohydrates	22g
Fiber	2g
Sugar	1g
Protein	6g

FOR THE BIRDS?

In the United States, millet is frequently used as a bird-friendly rice alternative at weddings and as a filler in bird feeders. But it's not just for birds. Millet is a healthy whole grain used widely in Africa and Asia. It's becoming more popular in the West because it's gluten-free and high in protein, fiber, and antioxidants.

Summer Squash and Barley Risotto

Fresh asparagus instead of summer squash would also be lovely in this nontraditional risotto. Top it off with some vegan Parmesan cheese.

SERVES 4

Per Serving:

Calories	302
Fat	10g
Sodium	994mg
Carbohydrates	47g
Fiber	10g
Sugar	5g
Protein	8g

2 tablespoons olive oil

4 cloves garlic, peeled and minced

1 small onion, peeled and diced

1 medium zucchini, trimmed and chopped

1 medium yellow squash, trimmed and chopped

1 cup uncooked pearled barley

3¼ cups vegetable broth

2 tablespoons chopped fresh basil

2 tablespoons nutritional yeast

2 tablespoons vegan margarine

½ teaspoon salt

½ teaspoon ground black pepper

1 In a large saucepan or Dutch oven, heat oil over medium heat. Add garlic, onion, zucchini, and yellow squash. Sauté 4–5 minutes until soft. Add barley and heat 1 minute, stirring to coat well with oil and to prevent burning.

2 Add 1 cup broth and stir to combine. Bring to a simmer. When most of the broth has been absorbed, add another ½ cup, stirring constantly. Continue adding broth ¼–½ cup at a time, stirring until most of liquid is absorbed after each addition, about 20 minutes, until barley is soft.

3 Stir in basil, yeast, margarine, salt, and pepper. Serve immediately.

Millet and Butternut Squash Casserole

Top this slightly sweet, slightly savory casserole with some Pan-Fried Tofu (see recipe in Chapter 6) to make it a main meal.

1 cup millet

2 cups vegetable broth

1 small butternut squash, peeled, seeded, and chopped

1 teaspoon curry powder

½ cup orange juice

2 tablespoons nutritional yeast

½ teaspoon salt

SERVES 4

Per Serving:

Calories	257
Fat	2g
Sodium	700mg
Carbohydrates	52g
Fiber	7g
Sugar	6g
Protein	8g

1 In a medium saucepan over high heat, combine millet and broth. Bring to a boil. Reduce heat to low, cover, and simmer until soft, 20–30 minutes.

2 Meanwhile, place squash in another medium saucepan over high heat and cover with water. Bring to a boil. Reduce heat to medium-low and simmer 10–15 minutes until squash is almost soft. Remove from heat and drain, then return squash to saucepan.

3 Add cooked millet, curry powder, and orange juice to squash and stir to combine. Cook over low heat 3–4 minutes. Stir in yeast and salt before serving.

Quinoa and Hummus Wrap

Lunch is the perfect time to fill up on whole grains. If you've got leftover tabbouleh, use that in place of the cooked quinoa.

1 (10") tortilla, warmed

3 tablespoons hummus

⅓ cup cooked white or red quinoa

½ teaspoon lemon juice

2 teaspoons Italian salad dressing

½ cup roasted red pepper strips

¼ cup sprouts

SERVES 1	
Per Serving:	
Calories	408
Fat	11g
Sodium	1,367mg
Carbohydrates	63g
Fiber	6g
Sugar	9g
Protein	12g

1 Place tortilla on a flat surface. Spread with hummus. Top with quinoa and drizzle with lemon juice and salad dressing.

2 Top with red pepper strips and sprouts. Roll tortilla into a cylinder shape, cut in half, and serve.

Quinoa with Dried Fruits

SERVES 4

Per Serving:

Calories	334
Fat	5g
Sodium	211mg
Carbohydrates	67g
Fiber	6g
Sugar	32g
Protein	7g

Cranberries and apricots make a sweet combo in this dish. Add some sage and thyme to give it some more warming flavors, and it would make an excellent Thanksgiving dish.

1 cup uncooked white or red quinoa

2 cups apple juice

1 cup water

2 tablespoons vegan margarine

1 small onion, peeled and diced

2 stalks celery, diced

½ teaspoon ground nutmeg

½ teaspoon ground cinnamon

¼ teaspoon ground cloves

½ cup dried cranberries

½ cup chopped dried apricots

1 teaspoon dried parsley

¼ teaspoon salt

1 In a large saucepan over high heat, combine quinoa, apple juice, and water. Bring to a boil. Reduce heat to medium-low, cover, and simmer 15 minutes. Remove from heat and fluff quinoa with a fork.

2 In a large skillet, melt margarine over medium-high heat. Add onion and celery and sauté 4–5 minutes until soft.

3 Add cooked quinoa, nutmeg, cinnamon, cloves, cranberries, apricots, parsley, and salt, tossing gently to combine. Reduce heat to low and cook 4 minutes. Serve hot or at room temperature.

Eggplant Puttanesca

Salty and garlicky puttanesca is a thick sauce traditionally served over pasta, but it's also good over brown rice.

2 tablespoons olive oil

3 cloves garlic, peeled and minced

1 medium red bell pepper, seeded and chopped

1 medium eggplant, trimmed and chopped

2 tablespoons capers

⅓ cup sliced Kalamata olives

½ teaspoon crushed red pepper flakes

1 (14.5-ounce) can diced tomatoes

1 tablespoon balsamic vinegar

½ teaspoon dried parsley

2 cups cooked brown rice

SERVES 4	
Per Serving:	
Calories	258
Fat	9g
Sodium	379mg
Carbohydrates	40g
Fiber	8g
Sugar	9g
Protein	5g

1 In a large skillet, heat oil over medium-high heat. Add garlic, bell pepper, and eggplant. Sauté 4–5 minutes until eggplant is almost soft. Add capers, olives, and red pepper flakes. Stir to combine.

2 Reduce heat to low and stir in tomatoes, vinegar, and parsley. Cover and simmer 10–12 minutes until juice from tomatoes has reduced.

3 Serve over rice.

CHAPTER 8

Classic Pastas

Easy Pad Thai Noodles

SERVES 4

Per Serving:

Calories	806
Fat	30g
Sodium	1,528mg
Carbohydrates	116g
Fiber	11g
Sugar	12g
Protein	24g

Volumes could be written about Thailand's national dish. It's sweet, sour, spicy, and salty all at once, and filled with as much texture and flavor as the streets of Bangkok themselves.

1 (16-ounce) package uncooked thin rice noodles (vermicelli)

¼ cup tahini

¼ cup ketchup

¼ cup soy sauce

2 tablespoons distilled white vinegar

3 tablespoons lime juice

2 tablespoons sugar

¾ teaspoon crushed red pepper flakes

¼ cup vegetable oil

1 (14-ounce) package firm or extra-firm tofu, drained, pressed, and diced

3 cloves garlic, peeled and chopped

¾ cup chopped scallions, divided

½ teaspoon salt

1 cup bean sprouts

¼ cup chopped roasted peanuts

1 small lime, sliced

1 Place noodles in a large bowl and cover with hot water. Set aside to soak about 5 minutes until soft.

2 In a small bowl, whisk together tahini, ketchup, soy sauce, vinegar, lime juice, sugar, and red pepper flakes.

3 In a large skillet or wok, heat oil over medium-high heat. Add tofu and garlic and stir-fry about 10 minutes until tofu is lightly golden brown.

4 Drain noodles and add to skillet. Stir-fry 3 minutes.

5 Reduce heat to medium and add tahini mixture, stirring well to combine. Cook and stir 3–4 minutes until heated through. Add ½ cup scallions and salt and cook 1 minute, stirring well.

6 Serve topped with remaining ¼ cup scallions, bean sprouts, peanuts, and lime slices.

White Lasagna with Spinach

This comforting, tasty lasagna is surprisingly easy to make. But your guests don't need to know that.

2 tablespoons olive oil

1 small onion, peeled and diced

4 cloves garlic, peeled and minced

1 (10-ounce) package frozen spinach, thawed and drained

½ teaspoon salt

1 (14-ounce) package firm tofu, drained, pressed, and crumbled

¾ cup Tropical Cashew Nut Butter (see recipe in Chapter 2)

2 cups unsweetened soy milk

1 tablespoon miso

2 tablespoons soy sauce

2 tablespoons lemon juice

3 tablespoons nutritional yeast

2 teaspoons onion powder

1 (16-ounce) package uncooked oven-ready lasagna noodles

SERVES 6

Per Serving:

Calories	762
Fat	36g
Sodium	802mg
Carbohydrates	80g
Fiber	8g
Sugar	8g
Protein	29g

1 In a large skillet, heat oil over medium-high heat. Add onion and garlic and sauté 4–5 minutes until soft. Stir in spinach and salt and cook about 2 minutes just until spinach is heated through. Stir in tofu and remove from heat to cool completely.

2 Meanwhile, in a small saucepan over low heat, combine Tropical Cashew Nut Butter, soy milk, miso, soy sauce, lemon juice, yeast, and onion powder. Cook, stirring, 1–2 minutes until smooth and creamy.

3 Preheat oven to 350°F. Lightly grease a 9" × 13" baking pan.

4 Ladle a thin layer of cashew sauce in prepared pan and spread to coat the bottom. Layer about one-third of noodles on top. Next add about one-third of spinach mixture and more sauce. Repeat layers until all ingredients are used up, ending with spinach and then sauce.

5 Bake 40 minutes. Cool at least 10 minutes before serving.

Zucchini and Basil Pomodoro

SERVES 4

Per Serving:

Calories	468
Fat	9g
Sodium	659mg
Carbohydrates	79g
Fiber	8g
Sugar	10g
Protein	16g

Pomodoro is a simple pasta dish with few ingredients. Make it in the late summer, when fresh, local tomatoes and zucchini are available.

2 tablespoons olive oil

2 large zucchini, trimmed and sliced

4 cloves garlic, peeled and minced

4 large tomatoes, cored and diced

⅓ cup chopped fresh basil

1 (12-ounce) package angel hair pasta or spaghetti, prepared according to package directions

½ teaspoon salt

¼ teaspoon ground black pepper

2 tablespoons vegan Parmesan cheese

1 In a large skillet, heat oil over low heat. Add zucchini and garlic and cook 1–2 minutes until zucchini is just soft. Add tomatoes and cook another 4–5 minutes. Transfer to a large bowl.

2 Add basil, pasta, salt, and pepper, and toss to combine. Serve topped with a sprinkle of vegan Parmesan.

Gnocchi with Walnut-Parsley Sauce

SERVES 4

Per Serving:

Calories	538
Fat	21g
Sodium	848mg
Carbohydrates	66g
Fiber	5g
Sugar	6g
Protein	16g

A simple and savory pasta sauce made with walnuts pairs perfectly with earthy potato gnocchi.

1 cup chopped walnuts

2½ cups unsweetened soy milk

2 tablespoons vegan margarine

2 tablespoons all-purpose flour

¾ teaspoon dried parsley

2 teaspoons nutritional yeast

½ teaspoon salt

¼ teaspoon ground black pepper

1 batch Garlic and Herb Gnocchi (see recipe in this chapter)

1 In a small saucepan over low heat, combine walnuts and soy milk. Cook 3–4 minutes to soften walnuts. Remove from heat and set aside.

2 In a separate small saucepan, melt margarine over low heat. Whisk in flour.

3 Slowly stir in walnut mixture. Heat, stirring constantly, 4–5 minutes until mixture thickens into a sauce.

4 Remove from heat. Stir in parsley, yeast, salt, and pepper. Pour over gnocchi and serve immediately.

Garlic and Herb Gnocchi

Homemade gnocchi are well worth the effort if you have the time. Serve with a simple Walnut-Parsley Sauce (see recipe in this chapter), or toss them with olive oil and freshly ground pepper to let the delicate herbal flavor shine through.

2 large russet potatoes
¾ teaspoon garlic powder
½ teaspoon dried basil
½ teaspoon dried parsley
¾ teaspoon salt
1½ cups all-purpose flour, divided

1 Preheat oven to 400°F.

2 Pierce potatoes two or three times with a fork and place directly on the oven rack. Bake about 50 minutes until soft. Remove from oven and set aside to cool 30 minutes. Peel potatoes and place in a large bowl.

3 Using a fork, mash potatoes with garlic powder, basil, parsley, and salt until completely smooth.

4 Sprinkle ¾ cup flour on a work surface and turn out potato mixture. Use your hands to work the flour into the potatoes to form a dough. Continue to add flour, a little at a time, using only as much as needed to form a dough. Knead about 5 minutes until smooth.

5 Divide dough into four equal portions. Roll each portion into a rope about 1" thick. Slice into 1"-long pieces and gently roll each piece against a fork to make grooves in the dough. Repeat with remaining dough.

6 Bring a large pot of water to a boil over high heat. Cook gnocchi in boiling water 2–3 minutes until they rise to the surface. Remove with a slotted spoon and serve immediately.

SERVES 4

Per Serving:

Calories	224
Fat	0g
Sodium	441mg
Carbohydrates	53g
Fiber	3g
Sugar	1g
Protein	7g

SERVING GNOCCHI

If you've made the effort to create fresh gnocchi, you want to taste the fresh pasta, so the sauce should be simple. Toss the gnocchi with vegan margarine or a flavored oil, then just sprinkle them with fresh herbs, salt, and pepper. Or try a combination of garlic and nutritional yeast

Chunky Vegetable Marinara

SERVES 4

Per Serving:

Calories	169
Fat	10g
Sodium	866mg
Carbohydrates	18g
Fiber	4g
Sugar	9g
Protein	3g

Toss in a handful of TVP or browned store-bought vegan beef crumbles for a "meatier" sauce. Pour this sauce over short pasta, such as ziti or rotini.

2 tablespoons olive oil

4 cloves garlic, peeled and minced

1 large carrot, peeled and thinly sliced

2 stalks celery, chopped

1 (28-ounce) can diced tomatoes

1 (6-ounce) can tomato paste

1 teaspoon dried oregano

1 teaspoon dried parsley

2 tablespoons chopped fresh basil

2 bay leaves

½ cup corn kernels

½ cup sliced black olives

1 tablespoon balsamic vinegar

½ teaspoon crushed red pepper flakes

½ teaspoon salt

1 In a large skillet, heat oil over medium-high heat. Add garlic, carrot, and celery. Sauté 4–5 minutes until softened.
2 Reduce heat to medium-low. Add tomatoes, tomato paste, oregano, parsley, basil, and bay leaves, stirring well to combine.
3 Cover and simmer 30 minutes, stirring frequently.
4 Add corn, olives, vinegar, red pepper flakes, and salt, and simmer 5 minutes.
5 Remove bay leaves before serving.

Artichoke and Olive Puttanesca

Use fresh basil and parsley if you have it on hand, but otherwise, dried is fine.

2 tablespoons olive oil

3 cloves garlic, peeled and minced

1 (14.5-ounce) can diced tomatoes

¼ cup sliced black olives

¼ cup sliced green olives

1 cup chopped artichoke hearts

2 tablespoons capers

½ teaspoon crushed red pepper flakes

½ teaspoon dried basil

¾ teaspoon dried parsley

¼ teaspoon salt

1 (16-ounce) package ziti pasta, prepared according to package directions

SERVES 6	
Per Serving:	
Calories	455
Fat	7g
Sodium	620mg
Carbohydrates	79g
Fiber	7g
Sugar	4g
Protein	15g

1 In a large skillet, heat oil over medium-high heat. Add garlic and sauté 1 minute. Add tomatoes, olives, artichokes, capers, red pepper flakes, basil, parsley, and salt. Bring to a boil.

2 Reduce heat to low and simmer 10–12 minutes until most of the liquid from tomatoes is absorbed.

3 Toss with pasta and serve hot.

Lemon, Basil, and Artichoke Pasta

A grooved pasta like rotini is perfect for catching this chunky sauce. The earthy rosemary, basil, and lemon flavors would also complement gnocchi well.

1 (16-ounce) package rotini, prepared according to package directions

1 (6-ounce) jar artichoke hearts, drained and chopped

2 large tomatoes, cored and chopped

½ cup minced fresh basil

½ cup sliced Kalamata olives

2 tablespoons olive oil

1 tablespoon lemon juice

½ teaspoon dried rosemary

2 tablespoons nutritional yeast

½ teaspoon salt

¼ teaspoon ground black pepper

1 In a large saucepan over low heat, combine all ingredients. Stir to mix well and cook 3–4 minutes until heated through.

2 Serve immediately.

SERVES 6

Per Serving:

Calories	387
Fat	8g
Sodium	368mg
Carbohydrates	63g
Fiber	6g
Sugar	3g
Protein	13g

Creamy Sun-Dried Tomato Pasta

SERVES 6

Per Serving:

Calories	380
Fat	5g
Sodium	273mg
Carbohydrates	64g
Fiber	5g
Sugar	2g
Protein	17g

CREAMY ROASTED PEPPER PASTA

You can make this sauce with roasted red peppers instead of sun-dried tomatoes. Or use a combination of the two.

Silken tofu makes a creamy, low-fat sauce base. If you're using dried tomatoes rather than oil-packed, be sure to rehydrate them well first.

1 (14-ounce) package silken tofu, drained

¼ cup unsweetened soy milk

2 tablespoons red wine vinegar

½ teaspoon garlic powder

½ teaspoon salt

1 (8-ounce) jar sun-dried tomatoes packed in oil, drained

1 teaspoon dried parsley

1 (16-ounce) package rotini pasta, prepared according to package directions

2 tablespoons chopped fresh basil

1 Place tofu, soy milk, vinegar, garlic powder, and salt in a blender or food processor and process until smooth and creamy. Add tomatoes and parsley and pulse until tomatoes are finely diced.

2 Transfer sauce to a small saucepan and heat over medium-low heat about 5 minutes until hot.

3 Pour sauce over cooked pasta and sprinkle with basil. Serve immediately.

Pumpkin Cream Pasta Sauce

This unusual mix of flavors and ingredients makes a simple but memorable sauce. Serve it over a short tubular pasta or use it in a lasagna or other baked pasta dish.

2 tablespoons vegan margarine

1 medium onion, peeled and chopped

2 cloves garlic, peeled and minced

1 (15-ounce) can pumpkin

1½ cups soy heavy cream

¼ cup nutritional yeast

½ teaspoon dried parsley

½ teaspoon salt

½ teaspoon ground black pepper

SERVES 4

Per Serving:

Calories	388
Fat	33g
Sodium	344mg
Carbohydrates	13g
Fiber	4g
Sugar	5g
Protein	4g

1 In a medium skillet, melt margarine over medium-high heat. Add onion and garlic and sauté 4–5 minutes until soft.

2 Stir in pumpkin and soy cream. Bring to a low simmer, reduce heat to low, and cook about 10 minutes, stirring frequently, until creamy.

3 Add yeast, parsley, salt, and pepper and simmer 2 minutes. Serve immediately.

Creamy Pasta and Peas

SERVES 6

Per Serving:

Calories	401
Fat	3g
Sodium	274mg
Carbohydrates	73g
Fiber	6g
Sugar	3g
Protein	17g

VEGAN WHITE SAUCE

Melted vegan margarine and soy milk form the base for many vegan cream sauces. Flour is the simplest thickener, but cornstarch or arrowroot also work. Garlic or onion powder and salt enhance the flavor, and nutritional yeast can be added for a cheesy flavor. When making a white sauce, use an unsweetened soy milk for a savory taste.

Replace the peas with frozen mixed vegetables, chopped broccoli, artichoke hearts, or any other vegetable you like.

½ cup unsweetened soy milk

1 teaspoon garlic powder

2 tablespoons vegan margarine

1 tablespoon all-purpose flour

1½ cups frozen peas, thawed

⅓ cup nutritional yeast

1 (16-ounce) package pasta shells, prepared according to package directions

½ teaspoon salt

½ teaspoon ground black pepper

1 In a medium saucepan over low heat, whisk together soy milk, garlic powder, and margarine. Add flour and cook 2–3 minutes, stirring constantly, until thickened.

2 Stir in peas and yeast and cook about 3 minutes until heated through. Pour over cooked pasta.

3 Season with salt and pepper before serving.

Sesame-Tahini Noodles

This is a creamy and nutty Chinese-inspired noodle dish. If you don't have Asian-style noodles on hand, spaghetti will do.

½ cup tahini

⅓ cup water

2 tablespoons soy sauce

1 clove garlic, peeled and diced

2 teaspoons minced fresh ginger

2 tablespoons rice vinegar

2 teaspoons sesame oil

1 medium red bell pepper, seeded and thinly sliced

3 medium scallions, trimmed and chopped

¾ cup chopped snow peas

2 (8-ounce) packages lo mein noodles, prepared according to package directions

¼ teaspoon crushed red pepper flakes

1 In a medium bowl, whisk together tahini, water, soy sauce, garlic, ginger, and vinegar.
2 In a large skillet, heat oil over medium heat. Add bell pepper, scallions, and snow peas. Sauté 2 minutes. Stir in tahini mixture and cooked noodles, stirring to combine.
3 Reduce heat to low and cook 2–3 minutes just until heated.
4 Sprinkle with red pepper flakes and serve.

SERVES 4

Per Serving:

Calories	660
Fat	18g
Sodium	467mg
Carbohydrates	99g
Fiber	9g
Sugar	4g
Protein	23g

Sweet and Spicy Peanut Noodles

SERVES 4

Per Serving:

Calories	505
Fat	15g
Sodium	786mg
Carbohydrates	81g
Fiber	5g
Sugar	11g
Protein	11g

These noodles entice you with their sweet pineapple flavor, then scorch your tongue with fiery chilies.

⅓ cup peanut butter

2 tablespoons soy sauce

⅔ cup pineapple juice

2 cloves garlic, peeled and minced

1 teaspoon grated fresh ginger

½ teaspoon salt

1 tablespoon olive oil

1 teaspoon sesame oil

2 small red chili peppers, seeded and minced

¾ cup diced fresh or drained canned pineapple

1 (12-ounce) package wide rice noodles, prepared according to package directions

1 In a small saucepan over low heat, stir together peanut butter, soy sauce, pineapple juice, garlic, ginger, and salt. Cook 2 minutes until well combined and smooth.

2 In a large skillet, heat olive oil and sesame oil over medium-high heat. Add chilies and pineapple and stir-fry 2–3 minutes until pineapple is lightly browned. Add cooked noodles and stir-fry 1 minute, stirring well.

3 Reduce heat to low and stir in peanut butter mixture. Heat 1 minute, stirring constantly. Serve immediately.

Orzo with White Wine and Mushrooms

Try using two different varieties of mushrooms for some extra color and depth of flavor.

2 tablespoons olive oil

1 cup sliced mushrooms

1 medium onion, peeled and chopped

3 cloves garlic, peeled and minced

1½ cups vegetable broth

½ cup white wine

1½ cups uncooked orzo pasta

2 tablespoons vegan margarine

2 tablespoons nutritional yeast

2 tablespoons chopped fresh basil

½ teaspoon salt

¼ teaspoon ground black pepper

SERVES 4

Per Serving:

Calories	357
Fat	10g
Sodium	637mg
Carbohydrates	53g
Fiber	3g
Sugar	5g
Protein	10g

1 In a large skillet, heat oil over medium-high heat. Add mushrooms, onion, and garlic. Sauté 3–4 minutes until just soft.

2 Add broth, wine, and orzo and bring to a boil. Reduce heat to low, cover, and simmer 8–10 minutes until orzo is cooked and liquid is absorbed.

3 Stir in margarine, yeast, basil, salt, and pepper. Serve immediately.

Stovetop "Mac 'n' Cheese"

SERVES 6

Per Serving:

Calories	427
Fat	11g
Sodium	491mg
Carbohydrates	66g
Fiber	5g
Sugar	2g
Protein	14g

The secret to getting this dish supercreamy and cheesy is using vegan cream cheese as well as vegan Cheddar. It's not particularly healthy, but it sure is delicious!

1 (16-ounce) package elbow macaroni pasta, cooked according to package directions

1 cup unsweetened soy milk

2 tablespoons vegan margarine

½ teaspoon onion powder

1 teaspoon garlic powder

½ cup vegan cream cheese

½ cup shredded vegan Cheddar cheese

⅓ cup nutritional yeast

½ teaspoon salt

¼ teaspoon ground black pepper

1 Drain cooked macaroni and place in a large pot over low heat. Stir in soy milk and margarine. Cook about 3 minutes until margarine is melted.

2 Add onion powder, garlic powder, cheeses, yeast, salt, and pepper. Cook 4–5 minutes, stirring constantly, until cheese is melted. Serve immediately.

Lemon-Thyme Orzo with Asparagus

The combination of lemon and thyme is understated and rustic; it smells and tastes good enough to bathe in. If asparagus isn't in season, use green peas or lightly steamed broccoli.

2 tablespoons olive oil

1 medium bunch asparagus, trimmed and chopped

1½ cups uncooked orzo pasta, prepared according to package directions

1 tablespoon grated lemon zest

2 tablespoons lemon juice

½ teaspoon salt

¼ teaspoon ground black pepper

2 teaspoons chopped fresh thyme

1 In a large skillet, heat oil over medium-high heat. Add asparagus and sauté 3–4 minutes until just tender. Do not overcook.

2 Add cooked orzo, lemon zest, lemon juice, salt, pepper, and thyme. Stir to combine and reduce heat to low. Cook 1–2 minutes, stirring constantly, until heated through. Serve warm.

SERVES 4

Per Serving:

Calories	297
Fat	8g
Sodium	291mg
Carbohydrates	50g
Fiber	4g
Sugar	3g
Protein	9g

Spaghetti with "Meatballs"

SERVES 6

Per Serving:

Calories	510
Fat	7g
Sodium	675mg
Carbohydrates	86g
Fiber	8g
Sugar	9g
Protein	21g

These little TVP nuggets are so chewy and addicting, you just might want to make a double batch. Don't be tempted to add extra water to the TVP; it needs to be a little dry for this recipe.

⅔ cup minced TVP

½ vegan beef-flavored bouillon cube

⅔ cup hot water

Vegan egg replacer equivalent to 2 eggs

1 small onion, peeled and minced

2 tablespoons ketchup

½ teaspoon garlic powder

1 teaspoon dried basil

1 teaspoon dried parsley

½ teaspoon ground sage

½ teaspoon salt

½ cup plain bread crumbs

⅔ cup all-purpose flour

2 tablespoons olive oil

3 cups marinara sauce

1 (16-ounce) package spaghetti, prepared according to package directions

1 Place TVP in a medium bowl. In a glass measuring cup, dissolve bouillon cube in hot water, then pour over TVP. Set aside 6–7 minutes until rehydrated. Gently squeeze out any excess moisture. Transfer to a large bowl.

2 Add egg replacer, onion, ketchup, garlic powder, basil, sage, and salt. Stir until well mixed.

3 Stir in bread crumbs. Add flour a few tablespoons at a time, mixing well until mixture is sticky and thick. You may need a little more or less than ⅔ cup flour.

4 Using lightly floured hands, shape the mixture into 1½"–2" balls.

5 In a large skillet, heat oil over medium heat. Pan-fry "meatballs," rolling them around in the pan to maintain the shape, 6–8 minutes until golden brown on all sides.

6 Reduce heat to medium-low and add marinara sauce. Simmer 5–7 minutes until thoroughly heated. Serve sauce and "meatballs" over cooked spaghetti.

Baked Macaroni and "Cheese"

SERVES 6

Per Serving:

Calories	524
Fat	8g
Sodium	523mg
Carbohydrates	85g
Fiber	6g
Sugar	5g
Protein	23g

Vegan chefs take pride in seeing who can create the best dairy-free macaroni and cheese ever. Join in the friendly rivalry with this recipe. Don't tell anyone that the silken tofu is the secret ingredient for the ultimate creaminess.

1 (16-ounce) package elbow macaroni pasta, prepared according to package directions

1 (14-ounce) package silken tofu, drained

1 cup unsweetened soy milk

2 tablespoons tahini

2 tablespoons lemon juice

1 tablespoon miso

1 teaspoon garlic powder

1 teaspoon onion powder

¼ cup nutritional yeast

2 tablespoons vegan margarine, melted

1 cup plain bread crumbs

¼ teaspoon ground nutmeg

½ teaspoon salt

½ teaspoon ground black pepper

1 Drain cooked macaroni and place in a large casserole or baking dish.

2 Preheat oven to 350°F.

3 Place tofu, soy milk, tahini, lemon juice, miso, garlic powder, onion powder, and yeast in a blender or food processor. Process until smooth and creamy, scraping the sides as needed. Pour tofu mixture over macaroni and toss to combine.

4 In a small bowl, combine margarine and bread crumbs. Stir to coat thoroughly. Spread bread crumb mixture on top of macaroni and sprinkle with nutmeg, salt, and pepper.

5 Bake 20–25 minutes until slightly crispy. Cool 5 minutes before serving.

CHAPTER 9

Miscellaneous Mains

Black Bean and Butternut Squash Chili

Squash is an excellent addition to vegan chili in this southwestern-style dish.

SERVES 4

Per Serving:

Calories	365
Fat	8g
Sodium	1,339mg
Carbohydrates	60g
Fiber	21g
Sugar	9g
Protein	16g

2 tablespoons vegetable oil

1 medium onion, peeled and chopped

3 cloves garlic, peeled and minced

1 medium butternut squash, peeled, seeded, and chopped into chunks

2 (15-ounce) cans black beans, drained and rinsed

1 (28-ounce) can diced tomatoes

¾ cup vegetable broth

1 tablespoon chili powder

1 teaspoon ground cumin

¼ teaspoon ground cayenne pepper

½ teaspoon salt

2 tablespoons chopped fresh cilantro

1 In a large saucepan or Dutch oven, heat oil over medium-high heat. Add onion and garlic and sauté 4–5 minutes until soft.

2 Add squash, beans, tomatoes, broth, chili powder, cumin, cayenne pepper, and salt. Stir to combine and bring to a boil.

3 Reduce heat to medium-low, cover, and simmer 25 minutes. Uncover and simmer another 5 minutes. Top with cilantro just before serving.

Eggplant "Parmesan"

Slowly baking these breaded eggplant cutlets brings out the best flavor, but they can also be pan-fried in a bit of oil.

1 medium eggplant, trimmed and cut into ¾" slices

½ teaspoon salt

¾ cup all-purpose flour

1 teaspoon garlic powder

⅔ cup unsweetened soy milk

Vegan egg replacer equivalent to 2 eggs

1½ cups plain bread crumbs

2 tablespoons Italian seasoning

¼ cup nutritional yeast

1½ cups marinara sauce

SERVES 4	
Per Serving:	
Calories	211
Fat	2g
Sodium	525mg
Carbohydrates	38g
Fiber	7g
Sugar	10g
Protein	9g

1 Place eggplant slices in a colander and sprinkle with salt. Set aside 10 minutes. Gently pat slices dry to remove extra moisture.

2 Preheat oven to 350°F. Lightly grease a medium casserole dish.

3 In a shallow bowl, combine flour and garlic powder. In another shallow bowl, whisk together soy milk and egg replacer. In a third bowl, combine bread crumbs, Italian seasoning, and yeast.

4 Coat each eggplant slice with flour, then carefully dip in soy milk mixture. Finally, press slices into bread crumb mixture and place in prepared casserole dish.

5 Bake 20 minutes. Remove from oven, top eggplant with marinara sauce, and return to oven about 5 minutes until sauce is hot. Serve immediately.

Caramelized Onion Pizza

Sweet onions and barbecue sauce are the perfect pair in this tofu-topped pizza.

3 tablespoons olive oil

2 large red onions, peeled and chopped

1 (14-ounce) package firm tofu, drained, pressed, and diced

⅔ cup barbecue sauce

1 (14-ounce) vegan pizza crust

½ cup diced fresh or drained canned pineapple

¼ teaspoon garlic powder

¼ teaspoon salt

½ teaspoon ground black pepper

1 In a large skillet, heat oil over medium heat. Add onions and sauté 8–10 minutes, stirring occasionally, until very soft. Add tofu and sauté another 10 minutes until tofu is lightly crisped and onions are soft and caramelized.

2 Preheat oven to 450°F. Spread barbecue sauce on pizza crust.

3 Top pizza with tofu, onions, and pineapple. Sprinkle with garlic powder, salt, and pepper.

4 Bake 12–14 minutes until browned, or according to instructions on pizza crust package. Serve immediately.

SERVES 4

Per Serving:

Calories	612
Fat	23g
Sodium	1,154mg
Carbohydrates	83g
Fiber	5g
Sugar	25g
Protein	16g

VEGAN PIZZA

You might be able to get vegan cheese at a pizzeria, but cheeseless pizza is more delicious than you might think. When ordering out, load your pizza with extra-flavorful toppings, and sprinkle it with nutritional yeast if you want that cheesy flavor.

Tofu and Portobello Enchiladas

SERVES 4

Per Serving:

Calories	556
Fat	22g
Sodium	1,927mg
Carbohydrates	72g
Fiber	8g
Sugar	15g
Protein	21g

GARDEN VEGETABLE ENCHILADAS

For a fresh-tasting variation of these enchiladas, omit the mushrooms and grate 3 carrots and 2 zucchini to use in the filling instead. Grated vegetables bake quickly, so you won't need to precook them.

Turn up the heat by adding some fresh minced or canned chilies. If you love vegan cheese, add a handful of grated cheese to the filling as well as on top.

2 tablespoons vegetable oil

1 (14-ounce) package firm tofu, drained, pressed, and diced

5 large portobello mushrooms, chopped

1 medium onion, peeled and diced

3 cloves garlic, peeled and minced

2 teaspoons chili powder

½ cup sliced Kalamata olives

1 (15-ounce) can enchilada sauce, divided

8 (8") flour tortillas

½ cup shredded vegan Cheddar cheese

1 Preheat oven to 350°F.
2 In a large skillet, heat oil over medium-high heat. Add tofu, mushrooms, onion, and garlic. Sauté 4–5 minutes until tofu is just lightly browned. Add chili powder and sauté 1 more minute.
3 Remove from heat and stir in olives and ⅓ cup enchilada sauce.
4 Spread a thin layer of the remaining enchilada sauce in the bottom of an 8" × 8" baking pan.
5 Place tortillas on a flat surface and spoon about ¼ cup tofu mixture in the center of each tortilla. Roll into cylinders and place them snugly in the baking dish. Top with remaining enchilada sauce and sprinkle with vegan Cheddar.
6 Bake 25–30 minutes until hot and bubbling. Serve immediately.

Squash and Lentil Curry

Red lentils complement the butternut squash and coconut best in this salty-sweet curry, but any kind will do. Look for frozen chopped squash to reduce the preparation time.

2 tablespoons olive oil

1 medium onion, peeled and chopped

2 cups chopped butternut squash

1 tablespoon curry powder

1 teaspoon ground cumin

2 small red chili peppers, seeded and minced

2 whole cloves

3 cups vegetable broth

1 cup dried red lentils

2 large tomatoes, cored and chopped

2 cups chopped fresh green beans

¾ cup canned coconut milk

2 cups cooked brown rice

SERVES 4

Per Serving:

Calories	521
Fat	17g
Sodium	624mg
Carbohydrates	77g
Fiber	13g
Sugar	9g
Protein	18g

1. In a large skillet, heat oil over medium-high heat. Add onion and squash and sauté 4–5 minutes until onion is soft. Add curry powder, cumin, chilies, and cloves. Sauté 1 more minute.
2. Add broth and lentils. Bring to a boil. Reduce heat to medium-low, cover, and simmer 10 minutes, stirring occasionally.
3. Remove lid and add tomatoes, green beans, and coconut milk, stirring well to combine. Simmer uncovered 4–5 more minutes, just until tomatoes and beans are cooked.
4. Serve over rice.

Polenta and Chili Casserole

SERVES 4

Per Serving:

Calories	412
Fat	5g
Sodium	1,148mg
Carbohydrates	74g
Fiber	18g
Sugar	10g
Protein	17g

Using canned chili and thawed frozen vegetables, this quick one-pot dinner needs just 10 minutes of prep time.

1 cup cornmeal

2½ cups water

2 tablespoons vegan margarine

3 (15-ounce) cans vegan chili

1 (12-ounce) bag frozen mixed vegetables (broccoli, cauliflower, and carrots), thawed

1 tablespoon chili powder

1 In a medium saucepan over medium-high heat, combine cornmeal and water. Bring to a boil, then reduce heat to low. Simmer 10 minutes, stirring frequently. Stir in margarine.

2 Preheat oven to 375°F. Spray a 9" × 13" baking dish with nonstick cooking spray.

3 In a large bowl, combine chili and vegetables. Transfer mixture to prepared baking dish.

4 Spread cornmeal mixture over chili mixture and sprinkle the top with chili powder. Bake 20–25 minutes until lightly browned. Serve hot.

The Easiest Black Bean Burger Recipe Ever

Veggie burgers are notorious for falling apart. If you're sick of crumbly burgers, try this simple method for making black bean patties.

1 (15-ounce) can black beans, drained and rinsed

3 tablespoons minced onion

1 teaspoon salt

1½ teaspoons garlic powder

2 teaspoons dried parsley

1 teaspoon chili powder

⅔ cup all-purpose flour

2 tablespoons vegetable oil

1 In a medium bowl, mash beans with a fork until slightly chunky. Add onion, salt, garlic powder, parsley, and chili powder, and mash to combine.

2 Stir in flour, a bit at time, until the mixture is firm but not crumbly. You may need a little bit more or less than ⅔ cup. Form mixture into six patties.

3 In a large skillet, heat oil over medium heat. Fry patties 3 minutes on each side. Patties will appear to be done on the outside while still a bit mushy on the inside, so fry them a few minutes longer than you think they need. Serve warm.

SERVES 6

Per Serving:

Calories	160
Fat	5g
Sodium	556mg
Carbohydrates	24g
Fiber	6g
Sugar	0g
Protein	6g

VEGGIE BURGER TIPS

If you have trouble with your veggie burgers crumbling, try adding egg replacer to bind the ingredients together, then chill the mixture before forming into patties. Veggie burger patties can be grilled, pan-fried, or baked, but they do tend to dry out a bit in the oven. If you want to bake them, make sure to add extra-juicy toppings, like tomatoes or sliced pickles.

Sweet Stuffed Butternut Squash

SERVES 4

Per Serving:

Calories	298
Fat	12g
Sodium	50mg
Carbohydrates	49g
Fiber	7g
Sugar	28g
Protein	3g

EASIER-TO-CUT SQUASH

Even the finest chef armed with the sharpest knife may have a bit of trouble cutting into a whole winter squash. To make the task easier, pierce the squash several times with a fork and microwave on high 3–4 minutes to soften it up a bit. Your knife will run through much easier afterward.

For a Thanksgiving side dish or a dinner party entrée that everyone will "ooh" and "ahh" over, try this stuffed squash. It looks beautiful, but it's super easy to prepare. Use raisins if you don't like cranberries.

2 small butternut squash, halved lengthwise and seeded

½ cup apple juice or orange juice

2 medium apples, cored and diced

½ cup chopped pecans or walnuts

⅓ cup frozen or fresh cranberries

¼ cup maple syrup

2 tablespoons vegan margarine, melted

½ teaspoon ground cinnamon

¼ teaspoon ground nutmeg

1 Preheat oven to 350°F.

2 Pour apple juice onto a rimmed baking sheet and place squash cut-side down on the sheet. Roast 20 minutes. Alternatively, you can microwave squash 10 minutes. Remove from oven.

3 In a large bowl, combine apples, nuts, and cranberries. Stir in syrup, margarine, cinnamon, and nutmeg, tossing to coat.

4 Stuff each squash half with apple mixture, piling any extra filling on top, and roast another 25 minutes. Serve immediately.

Black Bean Polenta Cakes

SERVES 4

Per Serving:

Calories	360
Fat	5g
Sodium	841mg
Carbohydrates	69g
Fiber	14g
Sugar	3g
Protein	12g

You'll love the southwestern flavors in this colorful confetti polenta loaf. Pan-fry individual slices if you like, or just enjoy it as it is.

1 (15-ounce) can black beans, drained and rinsed

6 cups water

2 cups cornmeal

1 small red or yellow bell pepper, seeded and diced

¾ teaspoon ground cumin

1 teaspoon chili powder

1 teaspoon garlic powder

¾ teaspoon dried oregano

½ teaspoon salt

½ teaspoon ground black pepper

2 tablespoons vegan margarine

½ cup bottled salsa

1 Lightly grease a 9" × 5" loaf pan.

2 In a medium bowl, mash beans with a fork until slightly chunky. Set aside.

3 In a large saucepan over high heat, bring water to a boil. Slowly add cornmeal, stirring constantly.

4 Reduce heat to low and simmer 10 minutes, stirring frequently and scraping the bottom of the pot to prevent sticking and burning.

5 Add bell pepper, cumin, chili powder, garlic powder, oregano, salt, and black pepper, and stir to combine. Continue to simmer, stirring frequently, for 10 minutes. Stir in margarine and beans.

6 Gently press mixture into prepared loaf pan, smoothing the top with the back of a spoon. Refrigerate at least 2 hours until firm. Slice and serve topped with salsa.

Vegan Pizza Bagels

Need a quick lunch or after-school snack for the kids? Pizza bagels to the rescue! For a real treat, top them with vegan "pepperoni" slices.

⅓ cup pizza sauce
½ teaspoon garlic powder
¼ teaspoon salt
½ teaspoon dried basil
½ teaspoon dried oregano
4 whole-wheat bagels, sliced in half
1 cup shredded vegan mozzarella cheese
¼ cup sliced mushrooms
¼ cup sliced black olives

1 Preheat oven to 325°F.
2 In a small bowl, combine pizza sauce, garlic powder, salt, basil, and oregano.
3 Place bagel halves on a large baking sheet. Spread sauce over each bagel half and top with vegan mozzarella, mushrooms, and olives.
4 Bake 8–10 minutes until cheese is melted. Serve immediately.

SERVES 4

Per Serving:

Calories	362
Fat	9g
Sodium	993mg
Carbohydrates	57g
Fiber	6g
Sugar	7g
Protein	12g

INDIVIDUAL PIZZAS

Flour tortillas (use two stacked together) and vegan pita bread also make easy crusts for individual pizza servings.

Chickpea Tacos

SERVES 6

Per Serving:

Calories	294
Fat	12g
Sodium	736mg
Carbohydrates	41g
Fiber	11g
Sugar	8g
Protein	9g

Canned chickpeas make an easy and healthy taco filling. Add some seasoned rice to the filling and wrap it in flour tortillas for burritos as well.

2 (15-ounce) cans chickpeas, drained and rinsed

½ cup water

1 (6-ounce) can tomato paste

1 tablespoon chili powder

1 teaspoon garlic powder

½ teaspoon onion powder

½ teaspoon ground cumin

¼ cup chopped fresh cilantro

6 (6") corn tortillas

½ medium head iceberg lettuce, cored and shredded

1 cup shredded vegan Cheddar cheese

½ cup vegan sour cream

½ cup sliced black olives

1 In a large skillet over medium-high heat, combine chickpeas, water, tomato paste, chili powder, garlic powder, onion powder, and cumin. Bring to a boil.

2 Reduce heat to medium-low, cover, and simmer 10 minutes, stirring occasionally. Uncover and simmer another 1–2 minutes until most of the liquid is absorbed. Stir in cilantro.

3 Spoon mixture into tortillas. Top with lettuce, vegan Cheddar, vegan sour cream, and olives. Fold in half and serve immediately.

Caramelized Onion and Mushroom Cheeseless Quesadillas

Sure, you can easily make vegan quesadillas using vegan cheese, but try this more nutritious version filled with a cheesy bean spread.

4 tablespoons olive oil, divided

1 small onion, peeled and chopped

1 cup sliced mushrooms

2 cloves garlic, peeled and minced

¼ teaspoon salt

½ teaspoon ground black pepper

1 (15-ounce) can cannellini beans, drained and rinsed

1 medium tomato, cored and quartered

3 tablespoons nutritional yeast

3 tablespoons lemon juice

½ teaspoon ground cumin

6 (10") flour tortillas

1 In a large skillet, heat 2 tablespoons oil over medium-high heat. Add onion, mushrooms, and garlic. Sauté about 8 minutes until onion and mushrooms are browned and caramelized. Sprinkle with salt and pepper.

2 Place beans, tomato, yeast, lemon juice, and cumin in a food processor or blender. Process until smooth.

3 Place three tortillas on a flat surface and spread each one with bean mixture. Top with onion mixture. Cover with remaining three tortillas.

4 In a large skillet, heat remaining 2 tablespoons oil over medium heat. Working in batches, fry quesadillas 2–3 minutes on each side until tortillas are lightly crispy. Serve immediately.

SERVES 6

Per Serving:	
Calories	375
Fat	14g
Sodium	742mg
Carbohydrates	52g
Fiber	6g
Sugar	5g
Protein	11g

"CHICKEN" QUESADILLAS

Add some store-bought vegan "chicken" strips to make heartier quesadillas for lunch or a light dinner. Or tuck in some jalapeño slices for an easy game day snack to serve with salsa and guacamole.

Easy Falafel

It's surprisingly easy to make falafel, and baking them means no stovetop mess from frying. Of course, if you prefer fried falafel, you can cook them in a few tablespoons of oil 5–6 minutes per side.

SERVES 4

Per Serving:

Calories	114
Fat	1g
Sodium	579mg
Carbohydrates	19g
Fiber	5g
Sugar	4g
Protein	6g

FALAFEL SANDWICHES

Stuff falafel into a vegan pita bread with some sliced tomatoes and lettuce. Top it off with a bit of tahini, tzatziki, or hummus for a delicious sandwich.

1 (15-ounce) can chickpeas, drained and rinsed

1 small onion, peeled and minced

1 tablespoon all-purpose flour

1 teaspoon ground cumin

¾ teaspoon garlic powder

¾ teaspoon salt

Vegan egg replacer equivalent to 1 egg

¼ cup chopped fresh parsley

2 tablespoons chopped fresh cilantro

1 Preheat oven to 375°F. Line a large baking sheet with parchment paper.
2 In a large bowl, mash chickpeas with a fork until slightly chunky.
3 Stir in remaining ingredients.
4 Shape mixture into 2" balls or 1"-thick patties and place on prepared baking sheet. Bake 15 minutes until crisp. Serve hot.

Olive and Artichoke Focaccia Pizza

This pizza is so flavorful, you won't even miss the cheese.

1 (12-ounce) loaf vegan focaccia bread

1 tablespoon olive oil

½ teaspoon salt

½ teaspoon dried rosemary

½ teaspoon dried basil

⅓ cup tomato paste

½ cup sliced green olives

¾ cup chopped artichoke hearts

½ cup sliced mushrooms

3 cloves garlic, peeled and minced

½ teaspoon dried parsley

¼ teaspoon dried oregano

½ teaspoon crushed red pepper flakes

1 Preheat oven to 400°F.
2 Place focaccia on a large baking sheet and drizzle with olive oil. Sprinkle with salt, rosemary, and basil.
3 Spread a thin layer of tomato paste on focaccia, then top with olives, artichoke hearts, mushrooms, and garlic.
4 Sprinkle with parsley, oregano, and red pepper flakes. Bake 20 minutes. Serve warm.

SERVES 3

Per Serving:	
Calories	405
Fat	16g
Sodium	1,971mg
Carbohydrates	52g
Fiber	6g
Sugar	7g
Protein	13g

FOCACCIA PIZZA

Sure, you could use a regular pizza crust for this recipe, but vegan food is all about maximum flavor, and focaccia has much more than a regular crust. If you do prefer a store-bought pizza crust, drizzle it with olive oil and herbs on both sides.

Baked Polenta with Italian Herbs

SERVES 2

Per Serving:

Calories	327
Fat	9g
Sodium	2,330mg
Carbohydrates	53g
Fiber	5g
Sugar	4g
Protein	7g

If you don't feel like spending time stirring polenta on the stove, bake it in the oven instead. Replace the dried herbs with fresh herbs if you have them. Serve the polenta warm or transfer it to a loaf pan, chill until firm, then slice and pan-fry it in a bit of oil.

1 cup cornmeal

4 cups vegetable broth

1 teaspoon dried parsley

¼ teaspoon ground sage

¼ teaspoon dried oregano

½ teaspoon salt

¼ teaspoon ground black pepper

1 tablespoon chopped fresh basil

3 tablespoons vegan margarine, melted

2 tablespoons nutritional yeast

1 Preheat oven to 450°F.
2 In a medium casserole dish, combine cornmeal and vegetable broth. Stir in parsley, sage, oregano, salt, and pepper.
3 Cover and bake 25 minutes. Uncover and bake another 5–10 minutes until liquid is mostly absorbed.
4 Stir in basil, margarine, and yeast. Serve warm.

Potato and Vegetable Fritters

These easy potato fritters are similar to an Indian snack called bajji or pakoras. Add a pinch or two of cumin, curry powder, turmeric, or garam masala for an Indian-inspired flavor.

3 medium red potatoes, peeled and cut into chunks

¼ cup unsweetened soy milk

⅓ cup all-purpose flour

½ teaspoon garlic powder

½ teaspoon onion powder

½ teaspoon chili powder

½ cup frozen mixed vegetables (peas, corn, and diced carrots)

½ teaspoon salt

¼ teaspoon ground black pepper

3 tablespoons vegetable oil

SERVES 4

Per Serving:

Calories	243
Fat	9g
Sodium	396mg
Carbohydrates	37g
Fiber	3g
Sugar	2g
Protein	5g

1 Place potatoes in a large saucepan and cover with water. Bring to a boil over medium-high heat and cook 15–20 minutes until tender. Drain and transfer potatoes to a large bowl. Set aside to cool at least 30 minutes.

2 Add soy milk, flour, garlic powder, onion powder, chili powder, mixed vegetables, salt, and pepper. Mash with a large fork or potato masher until mixture is thick and smooth.

3 Mixture should be dry but sticky. Add a little more flour or soy milk if necessary. Form mixture into four patties.

4 In a large skillet, heat oil over medium heat. Fry patties 3–4 minutes on each side until browned and crispy. Serve hot.

Portobello and Pepper Fajitas

Chopped seitan could take the place of the portobellos if you prefer, or look for vegan "steak" or "chicken" strips.

2 tablespoons olive oil

2 large portobello mushrooms, cut into strips

1 large green bell pepper, seeded and cut into strips

1 large red bell pepper, seeded and cut into strips

1 large onion, peeled and sliced

¾ teaspoon chili powder

¼ teaspoon ground cumin

⅛ teaspoon hot sauce

1 tablespoon chopped fresh cilantro

4 (8") flour tortillas, warmed

½ cup vegan sour cream

½ cup bottled salsa

1 medium avocado, peeled, pitted, and sliced

1 In a large skillet, heat oil over medium-high heat. Add mushrooms, bell peppers, and onion. Sauté 5 minutes.

2 Stir in chili powder, cumin, and hot sauce. Cook 2–3 more minutes until mushrooms and peppers are soft. Remove from heat and stir in cilantro.

3 Place tortillas on a flat surface and top with mushroom and pepper mixture. Roll tortillas into cylinder shapes and top each with vegan sour cream, salsa, and avocado slices. Serve immediately.

SERVES 4

Per Serving:

Calories	364
Fat	19g
Sodium	632mg
Carbohydrates	43g
Fiber	10g
Sugar	9g
Protein	7g

TIME-SAVING TIPS

Fresh is always best, but you can usually find frozen bell pepper strips ready to go in your grocer's freezer, and a vegan taco seasoning blend can take the place of the individual spices.

Sweet Potato Enchiladas

SWEET POTATO BURRITOS

Sweet potatoes and black beans make lovely vegan burritos as well as enchiladas. Omit the enchilada sauce and wrap the mixture in flour tortillas along with shredded lettuce, chopped tomatoes and onion, salsa, and anything else you like in burritos.

Enchiladas freeze well, so make a double batch to thaw and reheat for an easy lunch or dinner.

2 large sweet potatoes

1 small onion, peeled and minced

3 cloves garlic, peeled and minced

1 (15-ounce) can black beans, drained and rinsed

2 teaspoons lime juice

2 tablespoons canned sliced green chilies

2 teaspoons chili powder

1 teaspoon ground cumin

1 (15-ounce) can vegan green chili enchilada sauce

½ cup water

12 (6") corn tortillas

1 Preheat oven to 425°F. Line a baking sheet with foil.

2 Place sweet potatoes on baking sheet and prick all over with a fork. Bake 45–50 minutes until tender. Remove from oven and cool on a rack 5 minutes.

3 Reduce oven temperature to 350°F. Spray a large casserole dish with nonstick cooking spray.

4 Cut sweet potatoes in half and scoop flesh into a large bowl. Add onion, garlic, beans, lime juice, chilies, chili powder, and cumin. Stir until combined.

5 In a medium bowl, stir together enchilada sauce and water. Add ¼ cup of this mixture to the sweet potato mixture and stir to incorporate.

6 Spread about ⅓ cup enchilada sauce mixture in prepared casserole dish.

7 Place tortillas on a flat surface. Spoon about ⅓ cup sweet potato mixture in each tortilla, roll into cylinders, then place in the casserole dish.

8 Pour the remaining enchilada sauce mixture over the top of the rolled tortillas, being sure to coat all the edges and corners well.

9 Bake 25–30 minutes until sauce begins to bubble. Serve immediately.

Three-Bean Casserole

If you like baked beans, you'll like this bean casserole. It's an easy dinner you can get in the oven in just a few minutes.

1 (15-ounce) can vegan baked beans

1 (15-ounce) can black beans, drained and rinsed

1 (15-ounce) can kidney beans, drained and rinsed

1 medium onion, peeled and chopped

⅓ cup ketchup

3 tablespoons apple cider vinegar

⅓ cup light brown sugar

2 teaspoons mustard powder

2 teaspoons garlic powder

1 Preheat oven to 350°F.

2 Combine all ingredients in a large casserole dish.

3 Bake uncovered 55 minutes. Serve immediately.

SERVES 8

Per Serving:

Calories	204
Fat	0g
Sodium	531mg
Carbohydrates	42g
Fiber	8g
Sugar	17g
Protein	10g

Bell Peppers Stuffed with Couscous

SERVES 4

Per Serving:

Calories	255
Fat	7g
Sodium	57mg
Carbohydrates	41g
Fiber	6g
Sugar	6g
Protein	8g

Baked stuffed peppers are always a hit, and this recipe takes very little effort.

1¼ cups water

¾ cup uncooked couscous

2 tablespoons olive oil

2 tablespoons lemon juice

1 cup frozen peas, thawed

2 medium scallions, trimmed and sliced

½ teaspoon ground cumin

½ teaspoon chili powder

4 large green or red bell peppers

1 Preheat oven to 350°F.

2 In a medium saucepan over high heat, bring water to a boil. Stir in couscous, remove from heat, cover, and set aside 5 minutes. Fluff couscous with a fork and transfer to a large bowl.

3 Add oil, lemon juice, peas, scallions, cumin, and chili powder, and stir to combine.

4 Cut the tops off bell peppers and remove seeds. Reserve tops.

5 Place peppers upright in an 8" × 8" baking pan. Stuff couscous mixture into peppers and place the tops back on, using a toothpick to secure if needed.

6 Bake 15 minutes. Serve warm.

CHAPTER 10

Tofu

Cajun-Spiced Cornmeal-Breaded Tofu

SERVES 3

Per Serving:

Calories	180
Fat	6g
Sodium	345mg
Carbohydrates	20g
Fiber	3g
Sugar	2g
Protein	14g

This is a southern-inspired dish that recalls breaded and fried catfish. Serve it with hot sauce or barbecue sauce. For crisper tofu, fry it in vegetable oil 2–3 minutes on each side until golden brown instead of baking.

⅔ cup unsweetened soy milk

2 tablespoons lime juice

¼ cup all-purpose flour

⅓ cup cornmeal

1 tablespoon Cajun seasoning

1 teaspoon onion powder

½ teaspoon ground cayenne pepper

½ teaspoon salt

½ teaspoon ground black pepper

1 (14-ounce) package firm or extra-firm tofu, drained, pressed, and sliced into strips or triangles

1 Preheat oven to 375°F. Spray a large baking sheet with nonstick cooking spray.
2 In a wide, shallow bowl, combine soy milk and lime juice. In a separate shallow bowl, stir together flour, cornmeal, Cajun seasoning, onion powder, cayenne pepper, salt, and black pepper.
3 Dip tofu into soy milk mixture, then press into flour mixture. Place coated pieces on prepared baking sheet.
4 Bake 20 minutes, turning once halfway through cooking time. Serve warm.

Pineapple-Glazed Tofu

If you like sweet and sour dishes, you'll love this saucy, sweet, Pineapple-Glazed Tofu. Sauté some chopped vegetables with the tofu and toss it with noodles for a simple, satisfying meal.

½ cup pineapple preserves

2 tablespoons balsamic vinegar

2 tablespoons soy sauce

⅔ cup pineapple juice

3 tablespoons all-purpose flour

1 (14-ounce) package firm or extra-firm tofu, drained, pressed, and cubed

2 tablespoons vegetable oil

1 teaspoon cornstarch

2 teaspoons water

1 In a medium bowl, whisk together preserves, vinegar, soy sauce, and pineapple juice. Set aside.

2 Place flour in a shallow bowl. Coat tofu cubes in flour, then place on a platter or baking sheet.

3 In a large skillet, heat oil over medium-high heat. Add tofu and sauté 3–5 minutes until lightly golden. Stir in pineapple mixture and stir to coat tofu.

4 Reduce heat to low and cook 3 minutes, stirring frequently. In a small bowl, combine cornstarch and water. Add to skillet. Heat, stirring, 2 minutes until sauce thickens. Serve immediately.

SERVES 3

Per Serving:

Calories	369
Fat	14g
Sodium	620mg
Carbohydrates	48g
Fiber	2g
Sugar	28g
Protein	13g

Eggless Egg Salad

SERVES 4

Per Serving:

Calories	288
Fat	17g
Sodium	604mg
Carbohydrates	15g
Fiber	2g
Sugar	9g
Protein	19g

Vegan egg salad looks just like the real thing and is much quicker to make. Make sandwiches with it on toasted bread, or serve it on a bed of lettuce with tomato slices.

1 (14-ounce) package firm tofu, drained, pressed, and mashed with a fork

1 (14-ounce) package silken tofu, drained and mashed with a fork

½ cup Vegan Mayonnaise (see recipe in Chapter 2)

⅓ cup sweet pickle relish

¾ teaspoon apple cider vinegar

1 stalk celery, diced

2 tablespoons minced onion

1½ tablespoons Dijon mustard

2 tablespoons chopped chives

1 teaspoon paprika

1 Place mashed tofu in a medium bowl. Stir in Vegan Mayonnaise, relish, vinegar, celery, onion, mustard, and chives.

2 Cover and refrigerate at least 1 hour. Sprinkle with paprika just before serving.

Tofu Palak

Palak paneer is a popular Indian dish of creamed spinach and soft cheese. This version uses tofu instead of cheese.

2 tablespoons olive oil

3 cloves garlic, peeled and minced

1 (14-ounce) package firm or extra-firm tofu, drained, pressed, and cubed

2 tablespoons nutritional yeast

½ teaspoon onion powder

4 bunches fresh spinach, trimmed

3 tablespoons water

1 tablespoon curry powder

2 teaspoons ground cumin

½ teaspoon salt

½ cup plain soy yogurt

1 In a large skillet, heat oil over low heat. Add garlic and tofu and sauté 2 minutes. Stir in yeast and onion powder. Heat 2–3 minutes until tofu is lightly browned.

2 Add spinach, water, curry powder, cumin, and salt. Cook, stirring, 1–2 minutes until spinach wilts. Stir in yogurt and heat 1 minute more. Serve immediately.

SERVES 4

Per Serving:

Calories	226
Fat	12g
Sodium	509mg
Carbohydrates	16g
Fiber	8g
Sugar	3g
Protein	18g

TYPES OF TOFU

Made from cooked, coagulated soybeans and little else, tofu is a minimally processed, low-fat source of calcium and protein. Plain tofu comes in firm, extra-firm, or silken (also called silk or soft tofu), and many grocers stock a variety of prebaked or flavored tofu. Firm or extra-firm tofu is used in stir-fries and baked dishes when you want the tofu to hold shape. For creamy sauces, use silken tofu.

Tofu "Chicken" Nuggets

SERVES 4

Per Serving:

Calories	229
Fat	11g
Sodium	465mg
Carbohydrates	19g
Fiber	3g
Sugar	2g
Protein	13g

If your kids like chicken nuggets, try this tofu version with poultry seasoning instead.

¼ cup unsweetened soy milk

2 tablespoons prepared mustard

3 tablespoons nutritional yeast

½ cup plain bread crumbs

½ cup all-purpose flour

1 teaspoon poultry seasoning

1 teaspoon garlic powder

1 teaspoon onion powder

½ teaspoon salt

¼ teaspoon ground black pepper

1 (14-ounce) package firm or extra-firm tofu, drained, pressed, and sliced into thin strips

2 tablespoons vegetable oil

1 In a medium shallow bowl, whisk together soy milk, mustard, and yeast. In a separate shallow bowl, combine bread crumbs, flour, poultry seasoning, garlic powder, onion powder, salt, and pepper.

2 Coat each piece of tofu with the soy milk mixture, then press into bread crumb mixture. Place coated tofu on a platter or baking sheet.

3 In a large skillet, heat oil over medium-high heat. Add tofu strips and sauté 3–4 minutes on each side until lightly golden brown. Serve immediately.

Balsamic Baked Tofu

This sweet and crunchy baked tofu is delicious on its own or in salads or pastas. The extra marinade makes a great salad dressing.

1 tablespoon soy sauce

½ teaspoon sugar

¼ cup balsamic vinegar

½ teaspoon garlic powder

2 tablespoons olive oil

½ teaspoon dried parsley

½ teaspoon dried basil

¼ teaspoon dried thyme

¼ teaspoon salt

¼ teaspoon ground black pepper

2 (14-ounce) packages firm or extra-firm tofu, drained, pressed, and cut into ½" strips or triangles

1 In a medium bowl, whisk together soy sauce, sugar, vinegar, garlic powder, oil, parsley, basil, thyme, salt, and pepper. Transfer mixture to a large zip-top plastic bag. Add tofu, close bag, and shake gently to coat.

2 Marinate at least 1 hour.

3 Preheat oven to 400°F. Spray a large baking sheet well with nonstick cooking spray.

4 Place tofu on prepared baking sheet. Bake 15 minutes, turn over, then bake another 10 minutes. Serve immediately.

SERVES 3

Per Serving:	
Calories	290
Fat	19g
Sodium	523mg
Carbohydrates	10g
Fiber	3g
Sugar	6g
Protein	22g

PRESS, MARINATE, BAKE!

Now that you know how to make baked tofu, try creating your own marinades with your favorite spices and flavors. You can even use a store-bought salad dressing, teriyaki sauce, barbecue sauce, or steak marinade. Thicker dressings may need to be thinned with a bit of water first, and to get the best glazing action make sure there's a bit of sugar added.

Saucy Kung Pao Tofu

SERVES 6

Per Serving:

Calories	264
Fat	17g
Sodium	527mg
Carbohydrates	13g
Fiber	4g
Sugar	5g
Protein	16g

Try adding a few more vegetables to this flavorful dish, like bok choy, water chestnuts, or bamboo shoots. Serve it over noodles or rice.

3 tablespoons soy sauce

2 tablespoons rice vinegar or cooking sherry

1 tablespoon sesame oil

2 (14-ounce) packages firm or extra-firm tofu, drained, pressed, and cubed

2 tablespoons vegetable oil

1 large red bell pepper, seeded and chopped

1 large green bell pepper, seeded and chopped

⅔ cup sliced mushrooms

3 cloves garlic, peeled and minced

3 small red or green chili peppers, seeded and diced

1 teaspoon crushed red pepper flakes

1 teaspoon ground ginger

½ cup vegetable broth

½ teaspoon sugar

1½ teaspoons cornstarch

1 tablespoon water

2 scallions, trimmed and chopped

½ cup roasted peanuts

1 In a shallow baking dish, whisk together soy sauce, vinegar, and sesame oil. Add tofu and toss to coat. Marinate in the refrigerator at least 2 hours. Drain tofu, reserving marinade.

2 In a large skillet, heat vegetable oil over medium-high heat. Add bell peppers, mushrooms, garlic, chili peppers, and red pepper flakes. Sauté 3 minutes. Add tofu and sauté 1–2 minutes until vegetables are tender.

3 Add reserved marinade, ginger, broth, and sugar. In a small bowl, combine cornstarch with water. Stir into marinade mixture. Reduce heat to low and simmer 2 minutes, stirring constantly, until sauce thickens. Add scallions and peanuts and heat 1 minute. Serve immediately.

Lemon-Basil Tofu

SERVES 6

Per Serving:

Calories	162
Fat	12g
Sodium	224mg
Carbohydrates	4g
Fiber	1g
Sugar	2g
Protein	11g

Moist and chewy, this zesty baked tofu is reminiscent of lemon chicken. Serve it over steamed rice.

3 tablespoons lemon juice

1 tablespoon soy sauce

2 teaspoons apple cider vinegar

1 tablespoon Dijon mustard

¾ teaspoon sugar

3 tablespoons olive oil

3 tablespoons chopped fresh basil, divided

2 (14-ounce) packages firm or extra-firm tofu, drained, pressed, and cut into ½" slices

1 In a medium shallow baking dish, whisk together lemon juice, soy sauce, vinegar, mustard, sugar, oil, and 2 tablespoons basil. Add tofu and stir to coat. Marinate at least 1 hour.

2 Preheat oven to 350°F.

3 Place baking dish in oven and bake 15 minutes. Turn tofu slices, then bake another 10 minutes until done.

4 Sprinkle with remaining 1 tablespoon basil before serving.

Tofu Barbecue "Steaks"

These chewy tofu "steaks" have a hearty texture and a meaty flavor. They're delicious as is, or you can add them to sandwiches. If you've never cooked tofu before, this is a supereasy, foolproof recipe to start with.

⅓ cup barbecue sauce

¼ cup water

2 teaspoons balsamic vinegar

2 tablespoons soy sauce

1 tablespoon hot sauce

2 teaspoons sugar

2 tablespoons olive oil

1 small onion, peeled and chopped

2 (14-ounce) packages firm or extra-firm tofu, drained, pressed, and cut into strips

1 In a small bowl, whisk together barbecue sauce, water, vinegar, soy sauce, hot sauce, and sugar. Set aside.

2 In a large skillet, heat oil over medium-high heat. Add onion and sauté 4–5 minutes until soft, then carefully add tofu strips. Fry tofu about 2 minutes on each side until lightly golden brown.

3 Reduce heat to medium-low and add barbecue sauce mixture, stirring to coat. Cook 5–6 minutes until sauce absorbs and thickens. Serve hot.

SERVES 3

Per Serving:

Calories	347
Fat	19g
Sodium	1,098mg
Carbohydrates	24g
Fiber	3g
Sugar	17g
Protein	23g

TOFU VS. SEITAN

This recipe, like many pan-fried or stir-fried tofu recipes, will also work well with seitan, though seitan needs a bit longer to cook all the way through.

Braised Tofu Cacciatore

SERVES 4

Per Serving:

Calories	292
Fat	15g
Sodium	1,152mg
Carbohydrates	24g
Fiber	7g
Sugar	12g
Protein	21g

If you'd like a more "grown-up" Italian dish, use ½ cup white wine in place of ½ cup broth. Serve this over pasta, rice, farro, or polenta. It's also good spooned over baked potatoes.

2 tablespoons olive oil

1 medium onion, peeled and chopped

2 cups sliced mushrooms

1 large carrot, peeled and chopped

3 cloves garlic, peeled and minced

2 (14-ounce) packages firm or extra-firm tofu, drained, pressed, and cubed

1½ cups vegetable broth

1 (14.5-ounce) can diced tomatoes

1 (6-ounce) can tomato paste

1 bay leaf

½ teaspoon salt

1 teaspoon dried parsley

1 teaspoon dried basil

1 teaspoon dried oregano

1 In a large skillet, heat oil over medium-high heat. Add onion, mushrooms, carrot, garlic, and tofu. Sauté 5 minutes, stirring frequently.

2 Add broth, tomatoes, tomato paste, bay leaf, salt, parsley, basil, and oregano. Bring to a boil. Reduce heat to medium-low, cover, and simmer 20 minutes, stirring occasionally.

3 Remove bay leaf before serving.

Tofu "Ricotta" Manicotti

Check the label on the manicotti package—some need to be pre-cooked and some can be placed straight into the oven.

2 (14-ounce) packages firm tofu, drained, pressed, and crumbled

2 tablespoons lemon juice

2 tablespoons olive oil

2 tablespoons unsweetened soy milk

¼ cup nutritional yeast

½ teaspoon garlic powder

½ teaspoon onion powder

¼ teaspoon salt

1 teaspoon dried basil

2 tablespoons chopped fresh parsley

3 cups marinara sauce, divided

12 large manicotti, cooked according to package directions

⅓ cup grated vegan Parmesan cheese

1 Preheat oven to 350°F.
2 In a large bowl, mash together tofu, lemon juice, oil, soy milk, yeast, garlic powder, onion powder, salt, basil, and parsley until almost smooth.
3 Spread 1½ cups marinara sauce in a medium baking dish. Stuff manicotti noodles with tofu mixture and place filled pasta in baking dish.
4 Sprinkle with vegan Parmesan and cover with remaining 1½ cups sauce.
5 Cover and bake 30 minutes. Cool 5 minutes before serving.

SERVES 4

Per Serving:

Calories	479
Fat	18g
Sodium	784mg
Carbohydrates	55g
Fiber	8g
Sugar	8g
Protein	27g

SWITCH IT UP

If you can't find manicotti noodles (sometimes called cannelloni), use large pasta shells. Or cook some lasagna noodles al dente, then place the filling on top of a noodle and roll it up. Place seam-side down in a casserole dish, and stuff them in tightly to get them to stick together.

Sticky Teriyaki Tofu Cubes

STORING AND FREEZING TOFU

Freezing firm or extra-firm tofu creates a meatier and chewier texture, which some people prefer, and enables it to absorb sauces easier. After pressing tofu, seal in a zip-top plastic bag and freeze until solid. Thaw it just before using. If you don't use the whole block, cover leftover tofu with water and place in a sealed container. It will keep in the refrigerator up to 5 days.

Cut tofu into wide slabs or triangular cutlets for a main dish or smaller cubes to add to a salad. Small cubes are also perfect for an appetizer or snack.

⅓ cup soy sauce

3 tablespoons barbecue sauce

2 teaspoons hot sauce

¼ cup maple syrup

¾ teaspoon garlic powder

1 (14-ounce) package firm or extra-firm tofu, drained, pressed, and cubed

1 Preheat oven to 375°F.

2 In a medium shallow baking dish, whisk together soy sauce, barbecue sauce, hot sauce, syrup, and garlic powder. Add tofu and stir to coat.

3 Bake 35–40 minutes, tossing once, until browned. Serve hot or at room temperature.

Coconut Curried Tofu

Serve this spiced tofu over Coconut Rice (see recipe in Chapter 7).

1 tablespoon olive oil

1 (14-ounce) package firm or extra-firm tofu, drained, pressed, and cubed

2 teaspoons sesame oil

3 tablespoons peanut butter

2 tablespoons soy sauce

2 tablespoons water

1 teaspoon curry powder

¼ cup unsweetened coconut flakes

2 tablespoons minced fresh cilantro

1 In a large skillet, heat olive oil over medium heat. Add tofu and sauté 2–3 minutes until lightly golden brown.

2 Reduce heat to medium-low and stir in sesame oil, peanut butter, soy sauce, water, and curry powder. Heat, gently stirring to coat tofu, 5 minutes.

3 Add coconut flakes and cilantro and heat 1 more minute. Serve immediately.

SERVES 3

Per Serving:

Calories	305
Fat	24g
Sodium	604mg
Carbohydrates	9g
Fiber	4g
Sugar	3g
Protein	16g

Black Bean Taco Bowls

SERVES 2

Per Serving:

Calories	672
Fat	23g
Sodium	654mg
Carbohydrates	85g
Fiber	25g
Sugar	8g
Protein	38g

Versions of this filling dish are sold from street carts all over Mexico City.

2 tablespoons olive oil

1 (14-ounce) package firm tofu, drained, pressed, and diced

2 medium scallions, trimmed and chopped

1 cup frozen peas, thawed

1 cup frozen corn kernels, thawed

1 teaspoon chili powder

¼ teaspoon hot sauce

1 (15-ounce) can black beans, drained

4 (6") corn tortillas

1 In a medium skillet, heat oil over medium-high heat. Add tofu and scallions and sauté 3 minutes, then add peas, corn, chili powder, and hot sauce. Cook another 2 minutes, stirring frequently.

2 Stir in beans and reduce heat to medium-low. Simmer 4–5 minutes until heated through.

3 Place two corn tortillas in the bottom of two bowls. Top with tofu mixture and serve immediately.

Spicy Chili-Basil Tofu

This saucy stir-fry is a favorite in Thailand when made with chicken and fish sauce, but it can be made with soy sauce and tofu instead. Serve it with rice or rice noodles to soak up all the flavorful sauce.

2 tablespoons vegetable oil

4 cloves garlic, peeled and minced

5 small red or green chili peppers, seeded and diced

3 medium shallots, peeled and diced

1 (14-ounce) package firm tofu, drained, pressed, and cubed

¼ cup soy sauce

1 tablespoon vegan mushroom oyster sauce

1 teaspoon sugar

1 medium bunch Thai basil leaves

1 In a large skillet, heat oil over medium heat. Add garlic, chilies, and shallots. Sauté 3–4 minutes until fragrant and browned.

2 Add tofu and sauté 2–3 minutes until tofu is lightly golden brown.

3 Add soy sauce, mushroom oyster sauce, and sugar, stirring to combine and dissolve sugar. Heat 2 minutes, stirring frequently. Stir in basil and heat 1 minute until basil is wilted.

4 Serve immediately.

SERVES 3

Per Serving:

Calories	249
Fat	14g
Sodium	1,432mg
Carbohydrates	18g
Fiber	3g
Sugar	10g
Protein	15g

Nutty Pesto-Crusted Tofu

Make sure the basil leaves are completely dry before making these nutty, crispy, herbed tofu cutlets.

½ cup roasted cashews

½ cup fresh basil leaves, packed

3 cloves garlic, peeled

½ cup nutritional yeast

⅔ cup plain bread crumbs

½ teaspoon salt

¼ teaspoon ground black pepper

⅔ cup all-purpose flour

⅔ cup unsweetened soy milk

2 (14-ounce) packages firm or extra-firm tofu, drained, pressed, and cut into ¾"-thick triangles

¼ cup vegetable oil

1 Lightly grease a baking sheet.

2 In a blender or food processor, process cashews until coarse and fine but not powdery. Transfer to a shallow bowl. Clean and dry blender or food processor and process basil and garlic until finely minced. Add to bowl. Add yeast, bread crumbs, salt, and pepper.

3 Place flour in a separate shallow bowl and soy milk in a third bowl.

4 Using tongs, dip tofu cutlets in flour and turn to coat, then dip in soy milk. Next, coat with cashew mixture and transfer to prepared baking sheet.

5 In a large skillet, heat oil over medium heat. Fry tofu 2–3 minutes per side until lightly crispy. Serve immediately.

SERVES 3

Per Serving:

Calories	498
Fat	22g
Sodium	506mg
Carbohydrates	43g
Fiber	6g
Sugar	5g
Protein	35g

MAKE TOFU A STAPLE IN YOUR KITCHEN

Aside from the low cost and ease of preparation, tofu is beloved by vegans as an excellent source of protein, calcium, and iron. Plain sautéed tofu with a dash of salt is a quick addition to just about any meal, and many grocery stores offer premarinated and even prebaked tofu that is ready to go out of the package. What's not to love?

Lemon-Thyme Marinated Tofu

SERVES 3

Per Serving:

Calories	117
Fat	7g
Sodium	695mg
Carbohydrates	3g
Fiber	1g
Sugar	1g
Protein	11g

The leftover marinade can be whisked with some extra olive oil for a lemony salad dressing.

3 tablespoons lemon juice

3 tablespoons soy sauce

1 tablespoon olive oil

3 tablespoons water

1 tablespoon chopped fresh thyme

1 (14-ounce) package firm or extra-firm tofu, drained, pressed, and cubed

½ teaspoon salt

¼ teaspoon ground black pepper

1 In a medium shallow baking dish, whisk together lemon juice, soy sauce, oil, water, and thyme. Add tofu and stir to coat. Cover and marinate in the refrigerator at least 2 hours.

2 Preheat oven to 400°F. Spray a baking sheet with nonstick cooking spray.

3 Using tongs or a slotted spoon, transfer tofu to prepared baking sheet. Discard marinade. Sprinkle tofu with salt and pepper.

4 Bake 10–12 minutes until lightly crispy. Serve warm.

Five-Spice–Glazed Tofu

Chinese five-spice powder is a blend of spices with a unique taste. Use this spiced tofu in salads, stir-fries, and fried rice.

½ cup water

2 tablespoons soy sauce

1 tablespoon sesame oil

1 tablespoon light brown sugar

2 cloves garlic, peeled and minced

¾ teaspoon Chinese five-spice powder

1 (14-ounce) package firm tofu, drained, pressed, and cut into ½" slabs or triangles

SERVES 3

Per Serving:

Calories	158
Fat	10g
Sodium	602mg
Carbohydrates	8g
Fiber	2g
Sugar	5g
Protein	12g

1 In a medium shallow baking dish, whisk together water, soy sauce, oil, brown sugar, garlic, and five-spice powder. Add tofu and stir to coat. Cover and marinate at least 30 minutes.

2 Preheat oven to 350°F.

3 Place baking dish in oven and bake 10 minutes. Turn tofu and bake another 10 minutes. Serve warm.

Orange-Glazed Tofu

SERVES 3

Per Serving:

Calories	233
Fat	14g
Sodium	603mg
Carbohydrates	16g
Fiber	2g
Sugar	10g
Protein	12g

If you're missing Chinese restaurant–style orange-glazed chicken, try this easy tofu version. It's slightly sweet and slightly salty, and thanks to the red pepper flakes, it has a kick as well. Double the sauce and add some vegetables and rice for a full meal.

⅔ cup orange juice

2 tablespoons soy sauce

2 tablespoons rice vinegar

1 tablespoon maple syrup

½ teaspoon crushed red pepper flakes

2 tablespoons olive oil

1 (14-ounce) package firm or extra-firm tofu, drained, pressed, and cubed

3 cloves garlic, peeled and minced

1½ teaspoons cornstarch

2 tablespoons water

1 In a medium bowl, whisk together orange juice, soy sauce, vinegar, syrup, and red pepper flakes and set aside.

2 In a large skillet, heat oil over medium heat. Add tofu and garlic and sauté 2 minutes.

3 Stir in orange juice mixture, bring just to a simmer, and reduce heat to low. Simmer 8 minutes.

4 In a small bowl, whisk together cornstarch and water until cornstarch is dissolved. Add to tofu mixture and stir to combine.

5 Simmer 3–4 minutes until sauce thickens. Serve immediately.

CHAPTER 11
Seitan, TVP, and Tempeh

Vegan "Meatloaf"

SERVES 6

Per Serving:

Calories	402
Fat	4g
Sodium	914mg
Carbohydrates	43g
Fiber	7g
Sugar	17g
Protein	48g

With a slightly chewy texture, this "meatloaf" impersonates the real thing well. Top it with vegan gravy for a comforting dinner.

2 cups minced TVP

1¾ cups hot vegetable broth

1 tablespoon vegetable oil

1 medium onion, peeled and minced

¼ cup ketchup

⅓ cup plus 3 tablespoons barbecue sauce, divided

1 cup vital wheat gluten flour

1 cup plain bread crumbs

1 teaspoon dried parsley

½ teaspoon ground sage

½ teaspoon salt

¼ teaspoon ground black pepper

1. In a medium bowl, combine TVP with hot broth and set aside 6–7 minutes until rehydrated. Gently squeeze out any excess moisture.
2. In a medium skillet, heat oil over medium-high heat. Add onion and sauté 4–5 minutes until soft.
3. Preheat oven to 400°F. Lightly grease a 9" × 5" loaf pan.
4. In a large bowl, combine TVP, onion, ketchup, and ⅓ cup barbecue sauce. Stir in wheat gluten, bread crumbs, parsley, sage, salt, and pepper.
5. Gently press mixture into prepared pan and drizzle remaining 3 tablespoons barbecue sauce on top. Bake 45–50 minutes until lightly browned. Cool at least 10 minutes before serving.

Southern Fried Seitan

Deep-fried seitan is one the best things about eating vegan. Feel free to gloat when eating this amazing dish—those omnivores don't know what they're missing!

2 tablespoons soy sauce

¼ cup unsweetened soy milk

3 tablespoons prepared mustard

⅔ cup all-purpose flour

¼ cup nutritional yeast

1 tablespoon baking powder

1 teaspoon garlic powder

1 teaspoon onion powder

½ teaspoon paprika

½ teaspoon salt

½ teaspoon ground black pepper

1 (16-ounce) package traditional seitan slices

½ cup vegetable oil

SERVES 4

Per Serving:

Calories	350
Fat	18g
Sodium	1,389mg
Carbohydrates	22g
Fiber	3g
Sugar	2g
Protein	24g

1 In a medium shallow bowl, combine soy sauce, soy milk, and mustard. In a separate shallow bowl, combine flour, yeast, baking powder, garlic powder, onion powder, paprika, salt, and pepper.

2 Dip seitan pieces in soy milk mixture, then dredge in flour mixture. Place coated seitan on a platter or baking sheet.

3 In a large skillet, heat oil over medium-high heat. Line a large serving platter with paper towels.

4 Fry seitan pieces 2–3 minutes per side until golden brown. Transfer to lined platter to drain. Serve hot.

Homemade Seitan

Homemade seitan may seem like a lot of work at first, but it's quite simple once you get the hang of it, and it's just a fraction of the cost of store-bought seitan.

SERVES 8

Per Serving:

Calories	111
Fat	0g
Sodium	328mg
Carbohydrates	5g
Fiber	0g
Sugar	0g
Protein	22g

SEITAN TIPS

You can buy vital wheat gluten, also called wheat gluten flour, in the baking aisle or bulk section of many grocery stores. Note that this recipe is for a basic raw seitan. When using Homemade Seitan in a recipe, remember that it will expand when it cooks. Use more broth and a larger pot than you think you might need, and add a vegan bouillon cube for maximum flavor, if you like.

1 cup vital wheat gluten flour

1 teaspoon onion powder

1 teaspoon garlic powder

2 tablespoons soy sauce

6¾ cups vegetable broth, divided

1 In a medium bowl, combine wheat gluten, onion powder, and garlic powder. In a small bowl, stir together soy sauce and ¾ cup broth. Slowly add soy sauce mixture to wheat gluten mixture, mixing with your hands until all ingredients are incorporated.

2 Knead dough 2–3 minutes until smooth. Let dough rest a few minutes, then knead again 2 minutes.

3 Divide dough into four pieces. Stretch and press each piece to about 1" thickness.

4 In a large saucepan over high heat, bring remaining 6 cups broth to a boil. Add seitan pieces, reduce heat to low, and simmer 1 hour. Drain before using.

TVP Taco "Meat"

Whip up this meaty and economical taco filling in just a few minutes using prepared salsa, and have diners fill their own tortillas according to their taste. Nondairy sour cream, fresh tomatoes, shredded lettuce, and extra hot sauce are a must, as well as sliced avocados or vegan cheese if you have room.

2 cups minced TVP

2 cups hot water

2 tablespoons olive oil

1 medium onion, peeled and diced

1 small red bell pepper, seeded and diced

1 small green bell pepper, seeded and diced

2 teaspoons chili powder

1 teaspoon ground cumin

½ cup bottled salsa

½ teaspoon hot sauce

1 In a medium bowl, combine TVP with hot water and set aside 6–7 minutes until rehydrated. Gently squeeze out any excess moisture.

2 In a large skillet, heat oil over medium-high heat. Add onion and bell peppers and sauté 3 minutes. Add TVP, chili powder, and cumin. Cook, stirring frequently, 4–5 minutes until peppers and onion are soft.

3 Stir in salsa and hot sauce and remove from heat. Serve immediately.

SERVES 6

Per Serving:

Calories	169
Fat	5g
Sodium	196mg
Carbohydrates	14g
Fiber	7g
Sugar	7g
Protein	17g

TVP: AN INEXPENSIVE PROTEIN SOURCE

TVP is inexpensive and has such a meaty texture that many budget-conscious nonvegan cooks use it to stretch their dollar, adding it to homemade burgers and meatloaf. For the best deal, buy it in bulk. TVP is usually found in small minced crumbles, but some specialty shops also sell it in strips or chunks.

Seitan Buffalo "Wings"

SERVES 4

Per Serving:

Calories	374
Fat	20g
Sodium	1,066mg
Carbohydrates	23g
Fiber	2g
Sugar	2g
Protein	22g

BAKED, NOT FRIED

Admittedly, this is not the healthiest of vegan recipes, but you can cut some of the fat out by skipping the breading and deep-frying. Instead, lightly brown the seitan in a bit of oil, then coat with the sauce. Alternatively, bake the seitan with the sauce 25 minutes at 325°F.

To tame these spicy "wings," dip them in cooling Dairy-Free Ranch Dressing (see recipe in Chapter 4) and serve them with celery sticks and cucumber spears.

⅓ cup vegan margarine

⅓ cup hot sauce

1 cup all-purpose flour

1 teaspoon garlic powder

1 teaspoon onion powder

¼ teaspoon ground black pepper

½ cup unsweetened soy milk

2 cups vegetable oil

1 (16-ounce) package traditional seitan or mock chicken chunks

1 In a small saucepan over low heat, combine margarine and hot sauce and stir just until margarine is melted. Remove from heat and set aside.

2 In a shallow bowl, combine flour, garlic powder, onion powder, and pepper. Place soy milk in a separate shallow bowl.

3 In a large deep frying pan or Dutch oven, heat oil over medium-high heat. Line a large plate with paper towels.

4 Dip each seitan piece in soy milk, then dredge in flour mixture. Carefully place a few pieces in hot oil and fry 2–3 minutes per side until lightly golden brown. Transfer to lined plate. Continue with remaining seitan.

5 Transfer fried seitan to a large bowl and add reserved hot sauce mixture. Toss to coat and serve immediately.

Tandoori Seitan

SERVES 6

Per Serving:

Calories	164
Fat	5g
Sodium	644mg
Carbohydrates	14g
Fiber	3g
Sugar	5g
Protein	15g

You can enjoy the flavors of traditional Indian tandoori without firing up your grill by simmering the seitan on the stovetop.

⅔ cup soy yogurt

2 tablespoons lemon juice

1½ tablespoons tandoori spice blend

½ teaspoon ground cumin

½ teaspoon garlic powder

¼ teaspoon salt

1 (16-ounce) package traditional seitan, chopped

2 tablespoons vegetable oil

1 medium red bell pepper, seeded and chopped

1 medium onion, peeled and chopped

1 large tomato, cored and chopped

1 In a shallow baking dish, whisk together yogurt, lemon juice, tandoori spices, cumin, garlic powder, and salt. Add seitan and turn to coat. Marinate at least 1 hour.

2 With a slotted spoon, remove seitan from marinade. Reserve marinade.

3 In a large skillet, heat oil over medium heat. Add pepper, onion, and tomato. Sauté 3–4 minutes until just barely soft. Reduce heat to low and add seitan. Cook 10 minutes, tossing seitan occasionally.

4 Transfer seitan to a serving dish and drizzle with reserved marinade. Serve immediately.

Sweet and Sour Tempeh

With maple syrup instead of white sugar, this is a sweet and sour dish that's slightly less sweet than other versions. There's plenty of sauce, so plan on serving it with some rice or another grain to soak it all up.

1 cup vegetable broth

2 tablespoons soy sauce

1 (8-ounce) package original tempeh, cubed

2 tablespoons barbecue sauce

½ teaspoon ground ginger

2 tablespoons maple syrup

⅓ cup rice vinegar

1 tablespoon cornstarch

1 (15-ounce) can pineapple chunks, drained (reserve juice)

2 tablespoons olive oil

1 medium green bell pepper, seeded and chopped

1 medium red bell pepper, seeded and chopped

1 medium onion, peeled and chopped

2 cups cooked brown rice

1 In a large saucepan over high heat, combine broth and soy sauce and bring to a boil. Add tempeh and reduce heat to low. Simmer 10 minutes. Remove tempeh using a slotted spoon and set aside. Reserve ½ cup of the cooking liquid.

2 In a small bowl, whisk together barbecue sauce, ginger, maple syrup, vinegar, cornstarch, and pineapple juice. Set aside.

3 In a large skillet, heat oil over medium-high heat. Add tempeh, bell peppers, and onion. Sauté 3 minutes. Add barbecue sauce mixture and reserved tempeh cooking liquid and bring to a boil.

4 Reduce heat to low and simmer 6–8 minutes until sauce thickens. Stir in pineapple chunks. Serve over rice.

SERVES 4

Per Serving:

Calories	426
Fat	13g
Sodium	737mg
Carbohydrates	64g
Fiber	4g
Sugar	28g
Protein	15g

LIKE SWEET AND SOUR?

This sauce would go equally well with some sautéed tofu, lightly browned seitan, or any vegetables that you like.

Chickeny Seitan

SEITAN STYLINGS

When making home-made seitan, experiment with different seasonings to determine what you like best. You might add lemon juice and minced seaweed for a fishy taste, or try out different vegetable broths and bouillon flavorings.

Use a vegan chicken-flavored broth instead of regular vegetable broth, or add vegan chicken-flavored bouillon if you can find it.

1 cup vital wheat gluten flour

1 tablespoon nutritional yeast

½ teaspoon ground sage

¼ teaspoon dried thyme

½ teaspoon garlic powder

½ teaspoon onion powder

6¾ cups vegetable broth, divided

1 In a medium bowl, combine wheat gluten, yeast, sage, thyme, garlic powder, and onion powder. Slowly add ¾ cup broth, mixing with your hands until all ingredients are incorporated.

2 Knead dough 2–3 minutes until smooth. Let dough rest a few minutes, then knead again 2 minutes.

3 Divide dough into four pieces. Stretch and press each piece to about 1" thickness.

4 In a large saucepan over high heat, bring remaining 6 cups broth to a boil. Add seitan pieces, reduce heat to low, and simmer 1 hour. Drain and serve.

Crispy Tempeh Fries

Frying these tempeh sticks twice makes them extra crispy.

1 (8-ounce) package original tempeh, sliced into thin strips
½ teaspoon salt
½ teaspoon garlic powder
¼ cup vegetable oil
¼ teaspoon seasoning salt

1 Heat 1" water in a large skillet over high heat. Bring to a boil, then add tempeh strips. Reduce heat to low, cover, and simmer 10 minutes. Drain and transfer tempeh to a platter or baking sheet.

2 Sprinkle tempeh with salt and garlic powder. Line a separate platter or baking sheet with paper towels.

3 In a large skillet, heat oil over medium-high heat. Fry tempeh 2–3 minutes per side until crispy and browned. Transfer tempeh to lined plate to drain, and cool at least 30 minutes. Reserve cooking oil.

4 Reheat oil over medium-high heat and fry tempeh again 5 minutes. Season with seasoning salt and serve immediately.

SERVES 2

Per Serving:

Calories	322
Fat	21g
Sodium	836mg
Carbohydrates	11g
Fiber	0g
Sugar	0g
Protein	21g

SIMMERING TEMPEH

Most tempeh recipes will turn out better if your tempeh is simmered in a bit of water or vegetable broth first. This improves the digestibility of the tempeh, softens it up, and decreases the cooking time. And if you add some seasonings such as soy sauce, garlic powder, or some herbs, it will increase the flavor as well.

No Shepherd, No Sheep Pie

SERVES 6

Per Serving:

Calories	302
Fat	6g
Sodium	342mg
Carbohydrates	43g
Fiber	8g
Sugar	7g
Protein	17g

Sheep- and shepherd-less pie is a hearty vegan entrée for big appetites.

5 medium Yukon Gold potatoes, peeled and cut into chunks

2 tablespoons vegan margarine

3 tablespoons plus ½ cup unsweetened soy milk, divided

¼ teaspoon dried rosemary

¼ teaspoon ground sage

½ teaspoon paprika

½ teaspoon salt

¼ teaspoon ground black pepper

1½ cups minced TVP

1½ cups hot water

2 tablespoons olive oil

1 small onion, peeled and chopped

2 cloves garlic, peeled and minced

1 large carrot, peeled and thinly sliced

¾ cup sliced mushrooms

1 cup frozen peas, thawed

½ cup vegetable broth

1 tablespoon all-purpose flour

1 Preheat oven to 350°F.

2 Place potatoes in a large saucepan and cover with water. Bring to a boil over medium-high heat and cook 15–20 minutes until tender. Drain and transfer potatoes to a large bowl. Add margarine, 3 tablespoons soy milk, rosemary, sage, paprika, salt, and pepper and mash until smooth using an electric mixer on low speed or a potato masher. Set aside.

3 In a medium bowl, combine TVP with hot water and set aside 6–7 minutes until rehydrated. Gently squeeze out any excess moisture. Transfer to a large greased casserole dish.

4 Preheat oven to 350°F.

5 In a large skillet, heat oil over medium-high heat. Add onion, garlic, and carrot. Sauté 4–5 minutes until onion is soft. Add mushrooms, peas, broth, and remaining ½ cup soy milk. Stir in flour just until sauce thickens, then pour over TVP in the casserole dish.

6 Spread potato mixture over vegetables.

7 Bake 30–35 minutes until lightly browned on top. Cool 5 minutes before serving.

Pineapple Baked Beans

Add a kick to these saucy homemade vegan baked beans with a dash of ground cayenne pepper if you'd like.

1 cup minced TVP

1 cup hot water

2 (15-ounce) cans pinto beans, undrained

1 medium onion, peeled and diced

2/3 cup barbecue sauce

2 tablespoons prepared mustard

2 tablespoons light brown sugar

1 (8-ounce) can diced pineapple, drained

3/4 teaspoon salt

1/2 teaspoon ground black pepper

SERVES 4

Per Serving:

Calories	441
Fat	0g
Sodium	1,398mg
Carbohydrates	81g
Fiber	6g
Sugar	33g
Protein	26g

1 In a medium bowl, combine TVP with hot water and set aside 6–7 minutes until rehydrated. Gently squeeze out any excess moisture.

2 In a large saucepan over medium-high heat, combine beans and about half their liquid, onion, barbecue sauce, mustard, and brown sugar. Bring to a boil. Cover, reduce heat to low, and simmer 10 minutes, stirring occasionally.

3 Add TVP, pineapple, salt, and pepper to bean mixture. Cover and simmer another 10 minutes. Serve immediately.

Spicy Seitan Taco Filling

SERVES 6

Per Serving:

Calories	138
Fat	5g
Sodium	424mg
Carbohydrates	10g
Fiber	2g
Sugar	3g
Protein	14g

Finely dice the seitan or pulse it in a food processor so that the maximum surface area will come into contact with the spicy flavorings.

2 tablespoons vegetable oil

1 small onion, peeled and diced

½ medium green bell pepper, seeded and diced

1 large tomato, cored and chopped

1 (16-ounce) package traditional seitan, diced

1 tablespoon soy sauce

1 teaspoon hot sauce

2 teaspoons chili powder

½ teaspoon ground cumin

1 In a large skillet, heat oil over medium-high heat. Add onion, bell pepper, tomato, and seitan. Sauté, stirring frequently, 7–8 minutes until seitan is browned and tomato and pepper are soft.

2 Reduce heat to medium-low and add soy sauce, hot sauce, chili powder, and cumin, stirring to coat seitan well. Simmer 1 minute. Serve immediately.

Barbecue Seitan

Sooner or later, all vegans discover the magically delicious combination of seitan and barbecue sauce in some variation of this classic favorite.

2 tablespoons vegetable oil

1 (16-ounce) package traditional seitan, sliced into thin strips

1 large onion, peeled and chopped

3 cloves garlic, peeled and minced

1 cup barbecue sauce

2 tablespoons water

1 In a large skillet, heat oil over medium-high heat. Add seitan, onion, and garlic. Sauté 4–5 minutes until onion is soft and seitan is lightly browned.

2 Reduce heat to medium-low and stir in barbecue sauce and water. Simmer about 10 minutes until most of the liquid has been absorbed. Serve hot.

SERVES 6

Per Serving:

Calories	216
Fat	5g
Sodium	715mg
Carbohydrates	29g
Fiber	2g
Sugar	18g
Protein	14g

SEITAN SANDWICHES

Piled on top of sourdough along with some vegan mayonnaise, lettuce, and tomato, Barbecue Seitan makes a great sandwich. Melt some vegan cheese for a simple Philly "cheesesteak"–style sandwich, or add vegan Thousand Island dressing and sauerkraut for a seitan Reuben.

Seitan Gyros

These messy sandwiches have a huge cult following among street-food lovers. If raw onion isn't your thing, just leave it out.

2 tablespoons olive oil

1 (16-ounce) package traditional seitan, thinly sliced

¾ teaspoon paprika

½ teaspoon dried parsley

¼ teaspoon garlic powder

¼ teaspoon dried oregano

½ teaspoon salt

½ teaspoon ground black pepper

6 medium vegan pitas

2 small tomatoes, cored and thinly sliced

1 small onion, peeled and diced

½ medium head iceberg lettuce, cored and shredded

1 cup Vegan Tzatziki (see recipe in Chapter 2)

SERVES 6

Per Serving:

Calories	363
Fat	7g
Sodium	754mg
Carbohydrates	53g
Fiber	4g
Sugar	8g
Protein	22g

1 In a large skillet, heat oil over medium-high heat. Add seitan and sauté 2 minutes, then add paprika, parsley, garlic powder, oregano, salt, and pepper. Cook 5–7 minutes, stirring, until seitan is lightly browned and spices are fragrant.

2 Place pitas on a flat surface. Top each with seitan, tomato slices, onion, lettuce, and Vegan Tzatziki. Fold in half and serve immediately.

Vegan Chili Fries

SERVES 4

Per Serving:

Calories	654
Fat	17g
Sodium	2,022mg
Carbohydrates	90g
Fiber	21g
Sugar	19g
Protein	35g

Chili-cheese fries sin carne *(without meat) are (almost!) healthy enough to eat as an entrée. But go ahead and eat them for dinner. You deserve it, and no one will ever know.*

1 (20-ounce) bag frozen French fries

1½ cups minced TVP

1½ cups hot water

1 tablespoon vegetable oil

1 small onion, peeled and chopped

1 (15-ounce) can kidney beans, drained and rinsed

1⅓ cups tomato paste

2 tablespoons chili powder

½ teaspoon ground cumin

½ teaspoon ground cayenne pepper

2 tablespoons vegan margarine

2 tablespoons all-purpose flour

1½ cups unsweetened soy milk

2 tablespoons prepared mustard

½ teaspoon garlic powder

½ teaspoon salt

½ cup shredded vegan Cheddar cheese

1 Prepare French fries according to package instructions.

2 In a medium bowl, combine TVP with hot water and set aside 6–7 minutes until rehydrated. Gently squeeze out any excess moisture.

3 In a large skillet, heat oil over medium-high heat. Add onion and sauté 4–5 minutes until soft. Add TVP, beans, tomato paste, chili powder, cumin, and cayenne pepper. Bring to a boil. Cover, reduce heat to low, and simmer 10 minutes.

4 In a medium saucepan over medium heat, stir margarine and flour together until thick and pasty. Stir in soy milk, mustard, garlic powder, and salt. Add vegan Cheddar and heat just until melted and mixture has thickened.

5 Pile French fries on a large platter. Cover with TVP mixture and top with vegan cheese sauce. Serve immediately.

CHAPTER 12

Delicious Desserts

Pumpkin Maple Pie

SERVES 8

Per Serving:

Calories	201
Fat	5g
Sodium	253mg
Carbohydrates	34g
Fiber	2g
Sugar	24g
Protein	4g

CANDIED PECAN TOPPING

Make a sweet, buttery, nutty topping for your pie: Chop ½ cup pecan halves and mix with 2 tablespoons maple syrup, 2 tablespoons melted vegan margarine, and ⅛ teaspoon ground cloves, nutmeg, or cinnamon. Add to the top of the pie about halfway through the baking time.

Make the pie crust with gingersnap cookies to complement the fall spices in this classic American treat.

1 (16-ounce) can pumpkin

½ cup maple syrup

1 (12-ounce) package silken tofu, drained

¼ cup sugar

1½ teaspoons ground cinnamon

½ teaspoon ground ginger

½ teaspoon ground nutmeg

¼ teaspoon ground cloves

½ teaspoon salt

1 Vegan Cookie Pie Crust (see recipe in this chapter)

1 Preheat oven to 400°F.
2 Place pumpkin, maple syrup, and tofu in a food processor or blender and process until smooth and creamy. Add sugar, cinnamon, ginger, nutmeg, cloves, and salt. Pulse to combine.
3 Pour pumpkin mixture into pie crust.
4 Bake 1 hour. Cool at least 30 minutes before slicing and serving.

Mocha Ice Cream

If you have an ice cream maker, you can skip the stirring and freezing. Just add the blended ingredients to your machine and follow the manufacturer's instructions.

1 cup vegan chocolate chips

1 cup unsweetened soy milk

1 (12-ounce) package silken tofu, drained

⅓ cup sugar

2 tablespoons instant coffee

2 teaspoons vanilla extract

¼ teaspoon salt

SERVES 6	
Per Serving:	
Calories	312
Fat	15g
Sodium	132mg
Carbohydrates	35g
Fiber	3g
Sugar	28g
Protein	6g

1 In a small saucepan over very low heat or in the top of a double boiler, melt chocolate chips until smooth and creamy. Cool slightly.

2 Add soy milk, tofu, sugar, coffee, vanilla, and salt to a food processor or blender and process at least 2 minutes until very smooth and creamy. Add melted chocolate chips and process until smooth.

3 Transfer mixture to a 9" × 13" baking dish and place in the freezer.

4 Freeze about 4 hours, stirring every 30 minutes, until a smooth ice cream forms. If mixture gets too firm, transfer it to a food processor, pulse until smooth, then return to freezer.

Strawberry-Coconut Ice Cream

SERVES 6

Per Serving:

Calories	379
Fat	26g
Sodium	101mg
Carbohydrates	34g
Fiber	3g
Sugar	27g
Protein	3g

Rich and creamy, this is the most decadent dairy-free strawberry ice cream you'll ever taste.

2 cups canned coconut cream

1¾ cups frozen unsweetened strawberries

¾ cup sugar

2 teaspoons vanilla extract

¼ teaspoon salt

1 Add all ingredients to a food processor or blender. Process until smooth and creamy.
2 Transfer mixture to a 9" × 13" baking dish and place in the freezer.
3 Freeze about 4 hours, stirring every 30 minutes, until a smooth ice cream forms. If mixture gets too firm, transfer it to a food processor, pulse until smooth, then return to freezer.

Lemon Bars

SERVES 9

Per Serving:

Calories	368
Fat	9g
Sodium	287mg
Carbohydrates	68g
Fiber	2g
Sugar	44g
Protein	4g

HOMEMADE SWEETENED CONDENSED MILK

You can make your own nondairy sweetened condensed milk by combining 1 cup almond milk with ½ cup granulated sugar and 1 tablespoon cornstarch in a large microwave-safe bowl. Microwave mixture on high in 30-second intervals, stirring in between each interval, until thickened.

Enjoy the classic flavor of Lemon Bars in this vegan version. Dust some confectioners' sugar over them before serving if you like.

½ cup vegan margarine, softened
1 cup light brown sugar
¾ cup all-purpose flour
¾ cup whole-wheat flour
½ teaspoon salt
1 teaspoon baking powder
1 cup rolled oats
1¼ cups vegan sweetened condensed milk
½ cup lemon juice
1 tablespoon grated lemon zest

1 Preheat oven to 350°F. Line the bottom of a 9" × 13" baking pan with parchment paper.
2 In a large bowl, mix together margarine and brown sugar until well combined.
3 In a medium bowl, stir together both flours, salt, and baking powder. Add to margarine mixture and stir to combine. Stir in oats. Press half of the mixture into the bottom of prepared pan.
4 In a separate medium bowl, mix together condensed milk, lemon juice, and lemon zest. Spread over crumb mixture in pan. Top with remaining crumb mixture, but don't press down.
5 Bake 25 minutes until crumble is golden brown.
6 Cool in the pan on a wire rack 30 minutes. Cover pan with plastic wrap and refrigerate at least 1 hour.
7 Cut into bars and serve.

Coconut Rice Pudding

The combination of juicy, sweet mango with nutty coconut milk is simply heavenly, but if mangoes are unavailable, pineapples or strawberries would add a delicious touch to this creamy dessert.

1½ cups cooked white rice

1½ cups vanilla soy milk

1½ cups canned coconut milk

3 tablespoons brown rice syrup or maple syrup

2 tablespoons agave nectar

5 large dates, pitted and chopped

¼ teaspoon ground cinnamon

2 medium mangoes, peeled, pitted, and chopped

1   In a medium saucepan over low heat, combine rice, soy milk, and coconut milk. Bring to a very low simmer and cook 10 minutes, stirring occasionally, until mixture starts to thicken.

2   Stir in syrup, agave, and dates. Cook another 3 minutes, stirring constantly.

3   Remove from heat and set aside to cool at least 10 minutes. Scoop into small bowls, sprinkle with cinnamon, and top with mangoes. Serve warm or cold.

SERVES 4

Per Serving:

Calories	542
Fat	18g
Sodium	75mg
Carbohydrates	89g
Fiber	5g
Sugar	58g
Protein	7g

Maple Date Carrot Cake

SERVES 8

Per Serving:

Calories	269
Fat	4g
Sodium	413mg
Carbohydrates	61g
Fiber	4g
Sugar	49g
Protein	2g

EGG SUBSTITUTES

Commercial egg replacers are convenient, but ground flax meal works just as well. Whisk together 1 tablespoon flax meal with 2 tablespoons water for each "egg." Let it sit a few minutes and you'll see why it makes such a great binder, as it quickly becomes gooey and gelatinous. If you prefer a store-bought brand of egg replacer, Ener-G Egg Replacer is the most popular, but Bob's Red Mill works quite well too.

Made with applesauce and free of refined sugar, this is a cake you can feel good about eating for breakfast. Leave out the dates if you want to reduce the total natural sugar.

1½ cups raisins

1⅓ cups pineapple juice

6 large dates, pitted and diced

2¼ cups grated carrots

½ cup maple syrup

¼ cup applesauce

2 tablespoons canola oil

3 cups all-purpose flour

1½ teaspoons baking soda

½ teaspoon salt

1 teaspoon ground cinnamon

½ teaspoon ground allspice or ground nutmeg

Vegan egg replacer equivalent to 2 eggs

1 Preheat oven to 375°F. Grease and flour an 8" round cake pan.
2 In a large bowl, combine raisins and pineapple juice. Set aside 10 minutes.
3 Place dates in a small bowl and cover with water. Set aside 10 minutes. Drain water from dates, then add dates to raisin mixture. Add carrots, syrup, applesauce, and oil. Stir to combine.
4 In a medium bowl, combine flour, baking soda, salt, cinnamon, and allspice. Add to carrot mixture along with egg replacer. Stir to incorporate all ingredients.
5 Pour batter into prepared cake pan and bake 30 minutes or until a toothpick inserted in the center comes out clean. Cool in pan 5 minutes, then remove from pan and cool on a wire rack at least 30 minutes before serving.

Vegan Cookie Pie Crust

Use any kind of store-bought vegan cookie you like for this one: gingersnaps for pumpkin pies, chocolate or peanut butter sandwich cookies for cheesecakes, or vanilla wafers for a neutral flavor.

25 vegan vanilla wafer cookies
¼ cup vegan margarine, melted
½ teaspoon vanilla extract

1 Place cookies in a food processor and pulse until finely ground. Add margarine and vanilla and pulse just until the mixture comes together.

2 Press evenly into a 9" pie tin, spreading about ¼" thick. No prebaking is needed before using as a pie crust.

SERVES 8

Per Serving:

Calories	78
Fat	4g
Sodium	87mg
Carbohydrates	9g
Fiber	0g
Sugar	4g
Protein	0g

IT'S A GARNISH TOO

Plan on having a few extra tablespoons of this crumbly cookie mix to sprinkle on top of your pie or cheesecake for a sweet topping.

Cocoa-Nut-Coconut No-Bake Cookies

MAKES 24 COOKIES

Per Serving (1 cookie):

Calories	175
Fat	7g
Sodium	18mg
Carbohydrates	26g
Fiber	2g
Sugar	18g
Protein	3g

Have the kids help you shape these into little balls, and try not to eat them all along the way!

¼ cup vegan margarine

½ cup unsweetened soy milk

2 cups sugar

⅓ cup unsweetened cocoa powder

½ cup peanut butter

½ teaspoon vanilla extract

3 cups quick-cooking oats

½ cup finely chopped walnuts

½ cup unsweetened coconut flakes

1 Line a large baking sheet with waxed paper.

2 In a medium saucepan over medium-high heat, melt margarine. Stir in soy milk, sugar, and cocoa. Bring to a boil, stirring to dissolve sugar, then reduce heat to low. Add peanut butter and stir just until melted.

3 Remove from heat and stir in vanilla, oats, walnuts, and coconut. Set aside to cool 10 minutes.

4 Spoon about 3 tablespoons of batter at a time onto wax paper and press lightly to form a cookie shape. Refrigerate at least 2 hours or until firm before serving.

Pumpkin Pie Cupcakes

Add a handful of raisins or chopped walnuts if you like a little texture in your cupcakes, or frost them and garnish with fall-colored vegan candies.

1 (15.25-ounce) package vegan spice cake mix

1 (15-ounce) can pumpkin

¼ cup unsweetened soy milk

1 Preheat oven to 350°F. Lightly grease twenty-four muffin tin cups or line them with paper liners.

2 Combine all ingredients in a large bowl. Stir well to combine.

3 Fill muffin tin cups about ⅔ full and bake 12–15 minutes until a toothpick inserted in the center comes out clean. Cool in pans 5 minutes, then remove and cool on a wire rack at least 30 minutes before frosting and serving.

SERVES 24

Per Serving:

Calories	80
Fat	1g
Sodium	112mg
Carbohydrates	16g
Fiber	1g
Sugar	9g
Protein	1g

CHOCOLATE CUPCAKES

For a completely different flavor, use a vegan chocolate cake mix and add 1½ tablespoons unsweetened cocoa powder. Kick the chocolate flavor up a notch with a handful of vegan chocolate chips.

Chocolate–Peanut Butter Explosion Pie

This is a superrich, intensely chocolate dessert. Kids and adults alike will love it.

¾ cup vegan chocolate chips

1 (12-ounce) package silken tofu, drained

1¼ cups smooth peanut butter, divided

2 tablespoons plus ½ cup unsweetened soy milk, divided

1 Vegan Cookie Pie Crust (see recipe in this chapter)

2 cups confectioners' sugar

1 In a small saucepan over very low heat or in the top of a double boiler, melt chocolate chips.

2 Add tofu, ½ cup peanut butter, and 2 tablespoons soy milk to a food processor or blender. Process until combined, then add melted chocolate chips and pulse until smooth and creamy.

3 Pour into Vegan Cookie Pie Crust and refrigerate 2 hours until firm.

4 In a small saucepan over very low heat or in the top of a double boiler, combine remaining ¾ cup peanut butter, remaining ½ cup soy milk, and confectioners' sugar. Cook, stirring, 3–5 minutes until smooth and creamy. You may need a little more or less than 2 cups confectioners' sugar.

5 Spread peanut butter mixture over cooled pie. Refrigerate at least 1 hour before serving.

SERVES 8

Per Serving:

Calories	570
Fat	32g
Sodium	119mg
Carbohydrates	56g
Fiber	4g
Sugar	42g
Protein	14g

MAKE IT A LITTLE LESS INTENSE

This really is a rich chocolate and peanut butter flavor explosion, but if you want to tame it down a bit, it's still delicious without the peanut butter topping. Use sugar-free vegan chocolate chips or carob chips to make it even "healthier."

Vegan Peanut Butter Frosting

SERVES 8

Per Serving:

Calories	336
Fat	19g
Sodium	62mg
Carbohydrates	36g
Fiber	2g
Sugar	31g
Protein	7g

Kids will love this creamy frosting, and it's a nice change from the usual flavors, especially when paired with a chocolate cake.

1 cup peanut butter

⅓ cup vegan margarine, softened

2 tablespoons maple syrup

½ teaspoon vanilla extract

2 tablespoons unsweetened soy milk

2 cups confectioners' sugar

1 In a medium bowl, whisk together peanut butter, margarine, syrup, vanilla, and soy milk.

2 Slowly incorporate confectioners' sugar, using a little bit more or less to get the desired consistency. Use immediately.

Brownie Energy Bites

These energy bites may taste like brownies, but they deliver a punch of healthy ingredients like dates, walnuts, and flaxseeds.

1 cup pitted Medjool dates

½ cup rolled oats

1 cup walnut halves

¼ cup unsweetened cocoa powder

1 teaspoon vanilla extract

¼ cup unsweetened coconut flakes

¼ cup ground flaxseeds

¼ cup vegan chocolate chips

1 Add dates, oats, walnuts, cocoa powder, vanilla, coconut, and flaxseeds to a food processor. Pulse 3 seconds, then scrape down ingredients and pulse again until combined. Add chocolate chips and pulse two times to combine.

2 Roll dough into twenty bite-sized balls and place on a large baking sheet. Refrigerate 30 minutes before serving. Transfer leftover bites to a sealed container. Bites will keep up to 7 days in the refrigerator.

MAKES 20 BITES

Per Serving (1 bite):

Calories	110
Fat	6g
Sodium	1mg
Carbohydrates	14g
Fiber	3g
Sugar	10g
Protein	2g

Chocolate-Chia Pudding

SERVES 2

Per Serving:

Calories	423
Fat	15g
Sodium	96mg
Carbohydrates	69g
Fiber	17g
Sugar	47g
Protein	8g

This pudding is a rich, chocolate-infused dessert that satisfies your sweet tooth while meeting your health goals too.

2 tablespoons unsweetened cocoa powder

1 cup unsweetened almond milk

⅓ cup chia seeds

1 tablespoon vanilla extract

½ cup medium pitted Medjool dates

2 teaspoons chopped vegan dark chocolate chips

1 Add cocoa powder, almond milk, chia seeds, vanilla, and dates to a food processor. Pulse until smooth.
2 Transfer mixture to two small bowls. Cover and refrigerate at least 1 hour or up to 8 hours.
3 Sprinkle with chopped chocolate chips before serving.

Chocolate Chip Cookies

These are just like the cookies Mom used to make, only with a bit of applesauce to cut down on the fat.

⅔ cup vegan margarine, softened

⅔ cup granulated sugar

⅔ cup light brown sugar

⅓ cup applesauce

1½ teaspoons vanilla extract

Vegan egg replacer equivalent to 2 eggs

2½ cups all-purpose flour

1 teaspoon baking soda

½ teaspoon baking powder

1 teaspoon salt

⅔ cup quick-cooking oats

1½ cups vegan chocolate chips

1 Preheat oven to 375°F. Line two large baking sheets with parchment paper.
2 In the bowl of a stand mixer on medium speed, cream together margarine and granulated sugar. Add brown sugar, applesauce, vanilla, and egg replacer. Beat until smooth.
3 In a separate medium bowl, combine flour, baking soda, baking powder, and salt. Gradually add flour mixture to sugar mixture and mix until incorporated.
4 Fold in oats and chocolate chips.
5 Drop by generous spoonfuls onto prepared baking sheets 2" apart. Bake 10–12 minutes until golden brown. Cool cookies on a wire rack at least 10 minutes before serving.

MAKES 24 COOKIES

Per Serving (1 cookie):

Calories	207
Fat	7g
Sodium	150mg
Carbohydrates	32g
Fiber	2g
Sugar	18g
Protein	2g

WHITE CHOCOLATE MACADAMIA COOKIES

Swap out the vegan chocolate chips for vegan white chocolate chips and add ¾ cup chopped macadamia nuts for a heavenly grown-up version of this family favorite.

Vegan Vanilla Icing

Add a few drops of a flavoring extract or food coloring, or just use it as is.

¼ cup unsweetened soy milk

⅓ cup vegan margarine, softened

2 teaspoons vanilla extract

3 cups confectioners' sugar

Per Serving:

Calories	183
Fat	3g
Sodium	58mg
Carbohydrates	38g
Fiber	0g
Sugar	37g
Protein	0g

1 In a medium bowl, whisk together soy milk, margarine, and vanilla until smooth.
2 Slowly incorporate confectioners' sugar, using a little bit more or less to get the desired consistency. Use immediately.

FROSTING TIPS

Use an electric mixer to make this frosting super-light and creamy. Frosting will firm as it cools, so wait until cakes and cupcakes are completely cooled before frosting. Otherwise the heat will melt the icing.

Chewy Oatmeal-Raisin Cookies

The addition of applesauce makes these classic, nostalgic cookies superchewy. No egg replacer is needed.

⅓ cup vegan margarine, softened

½ cup light brown sugar

¼ cup granulated sugar

⅓ cup applesauce

1 teaspoon vanilla extract

2 tablespoons unsweetened soy milk

¾ cup whole-wheat flour

½ teaspoon baking soda

½ teaspoon ground cinnamon

½ teaspoon ground ginger

1¾ cups quick-cooking oats

⅔ cup raisins

MAKES 18 COOKIES

Per Serving (1 cookie):

Calories	117
Fat	2g
Sodium	62mg
Carbohydrates	24g
Fiber	2g
Sugar	13g
Protein	2g

1 Preheat oven to 350°F.

2 In the bowl of a stand mixer on medium speed, cream together margarine, brown sugar, and granulated sugar until smooth and creamy. Add applesauce, vanilla, and soy milk. Beat to combine.

3 Sift flour, baking soda, cinnamon, and ginger into a small bowl, then add to margarine mixture. Fold in oats and raisins.

4 Drop by generous spoonfuls 2" apart onto two large baking sheets.

5 Bake 10 minutes. Cool cookies on a wire rack at least 10 minutes before serving.

Raspberry-Lemon Cupcakes

SERVES 18

Per Serving:

Calories	207
Fat	5g
Sodium	226mg
Carbohydrates	37g
Fiber	1g
Sugar	24g
Protein	2g

Add ½ teaspoon lemon extract for extra lemony goodness in these sweet and tart cupcakes. Or omit the raspberries and add 3 tablespoons poppy seeds for lemon poppy seed cupcakes.

½ cup plus 6 tablespoons softened vegan margarine, divided

1 cup granulated sugar

½ teaspoon vanilla extract

⅔ cup unsweetened soy milk

3 tablespoons lemon juice

2 tablespoons grated lemon zest

1¾ cups all-purpose flour

1½ teaspoons baking powder

½ teaspoon baking soda

¼ teaspoon salt

¾ cup chopped raspberries

4 ounces vegan cream cheese, softened

½ cup raspberry jam

1½ cups confectioners' sugar

1 Preheat oven to 350°F. Grease eighteen muffin tin cups or line them with paper liners.

2 In the bowl of a stand mixer on medium speed, cream together ½ cup margarine and granulated sugar until light and fluffy. Add vanilla, soy milk, lemon juice, and lemon zest. Beat until combined.

3 In a medium bowl, sift together flour, baking powder, baking soda, and salt.

4 Add flour mixture to margarine mixture and beat just until combined. Do not overmix. Gently fold in raspberries.

5 Fill muffin tins about ⅔ full with batter and bake 16–18 minutes or until a toothpick inserted into a cupcake comes out clean.

6 Place muffin tins on a rack and cool 5 minutes, then remove cupcakes from tin and cool on the rack for at least 20 minutes.

7 In a medium bowl, beat together vegan cream cheese, jam, and remaining 6 tablespoons margarine. Gradually add confectioners' sugar and beat until smooth and creamy. Spread over cooled cupcakes and serve.

Mocha Frosting

SERVES 8

Per Serving:

Calories	188
Fat	4g
Sodium	55mg
Carbohydrates	40g
Fiber	1g
Sugar	37g
Protein	1g

The combination of chocolate and coffee in a frosting adds an elegant touch to even a simple cake-mix cake.

¼ cup strong coffee or espresso, cooled
⅓ cup vegan margarine, softened
2 teaspoons vanilla extract
⅓ cup unsweetened cocoa powder
3 cups confectioners' sugar

1 In a medium bowl, whisk together coffee, margarine, and vanilla until smooth. Stir in cocoa powder.
2 Slowly incorporate confectioners' sugar, using a little bit more or less to get the desired consistency. Use immediately.

STANDARD **US/METRIC**
MEASUREMENT CONVERSIONS

VOLUME CONVERSIONS

US Volume Measure	Metric Equivalent
⅛ teaspoon	0.5 milliliter
¼ teaspoon	1 milliliter
½ teaspoon	2 milliliters
1 teaspoon	5 milliliters
½ tablespoon	7 milliliters
1 tablespoon (3 teaspoons)	15 milliliters
2 tablespoons (1 fluid ounce)	30 milliliters
¼ cup (4 tablespoons)	60 milliliters
⅓ cup	90 milliliters
½ cup (4 fluid ounces)	125 milliliters
⅔ cup	160 milliliters
¾ cup (6 fluid ounces)	180 milliliters
1 cup (16 tablespoons)	250 milliliters
1 pint (2 cups)	500 milliliters
1 quart (4 cups)	1 liter (about)

WEIGHT CONVERSIONS

US Weight Measure	Metric Equivalent
½ ounce	15 grams
1 ounce	30 grams
2 ounces	60 grams
3 ounces	85 grams
¼ pound (4 ounces)	115 grams
½ pound (8 ounces)	225 grams
¾ pound (12 ounces)	340 grams
1 pound (16 ounces)	454 grams

OVEN TEMPERATURE CONVERSIONS

Degrees Fahrenheit	Degrees Celsius
200 degrees F	95 degrees C
250 degrees F	120 degrees C
275 degrees F	135 degrees C
300 degrees F	150 degrees C
325 degrees F	160 degrees C
350 degrees F	180 degrees C
375 degrees F	190 degrees C
400 degrees F	205 degrees C
425 degrees F	220 degrees C
450 degrees F	230 degrees C

BAKING PAN SIZES

American	Metric
8 × 1½ inch round baking pan	20 × 4 cm cake tin
9 × 1½ inch round baking pan	23 × 3.5 cm cake tin
11 × 7 × 1½ inch baking pan	28 × 18 × 4 cm baking tin
13 × 9 × 2 inch baking pan	30 × 20 × 5 cm baking tin
2 quart rectangular baking dish	30 × 20 × 3 cm baking tin
15 × 10 × 2 inch baking pan	30 × 25 × 2 cm baking tin (Swiss roll tin)
9 inch pie plate	22 × 4 or 23 × 4 cm pie plate
7 or 8 inch springform pan	18 or 20 cm springform or loose bottom cake tin
9 × 5 × 3 inch loaf pan	23 × 13 × 7 cm or 2 lb narrow loaf or pate tin
1½ quart casserole	1.5 liter casserole
2 quart casserole	2 liter casserole

Index

200 Delicious, Plant-Based Recipes Perfect for Weekly Meal Prep!

PICK UP OR DOWNLOAD YOUR COPY TODAY!